About the author

For the past 20 years, Graham Andrews has had an interest in personal development and self-motivation. In that time, he has motivate numerous others to achieve their goals through the use of creative imagery. Graham is a freelance writer, writing tutor and scientific editor. He is the author of ten books.

By the same author

A Guide To Wrought Iron And Welding

You're On Air

Easy Guide To Creative Writing

Easy Guide To Writing Winning Essays

Easy Guide To Science and Technical Writing

Island Of The Barking Dog

Dad Kept Bees

Reach For the Sky

Practical Arc Welding

In Your New Image

Using visualisation to guide you through the
changes you want to achieve in your own life

Graham J Andrews

Flairnet

Copyright © Graham J Andrews 2013

ISBN ISBN: 978-0-9875092-8-4

Published by Flairnet

www.flairnet.com.au
Post Office Box 645
Narooma NSW 2546
Australia

This book is copyright. Apart from any fair dealing for the purpose of private study, research or review, as permitted under the Copyright Act, no part may be reproduced by any process without written permission. Inquiries concerning publication, translation or recording rights should be addressed to the publisher.

National Library of Australia Cataloguing-in-Publication entry
Author: Andrews, Graham J., Author.

Title: In your new image : using visualisation to guide you through the changes you want to achieve in your own life / Graham J. Andrews.

ISBN: 9780987509284 (paperback)

Notes: Includes index.

Subjects: Self-actualization (Psychology)
Visualization.
Imagery (Psychology)

Dewey Number: 158.1

Contact the author:
Website: www.grahamandrews.com
Email: graham@grahamandrews.com

Contents

Introduction	7
Chapter 1 What's It All About?	13
Chapter 2 How It Works	39
Chapter 3 Visualisation	49
Chapter 4 Your Self Image	67
Chapter 5 Removing Anxiety	81
Chapter 6 Accepting Ourselves	104
Chapter 7 Dealing With Difficult People	110
Chapter 8 Acquiring New Skills	116
Chapter 9 Work	129
Chapter 10 Making Friends	158
Chapter 11 Feeling Good	164
Chapter 12 Being a Winner	176
Chapter 13 Where To From Here?	191
Index	193

Introduction

Many people would like to change some aspect of their behaviour. They want to learn a new skill or improve their sports ability. They would like to change the way they see themselves, or how they believe others perceive them. It's not always easy to change habits that have been with us for years, even decades.

The health industry costs billions of dollars every year. Part of that cost is attributed to the fact that people want to feel better about themselves and look nicer. Hypnosis can be effective in acquiring many desired changes. Self-hypnosis is also effective in a number of cases.

But so is visualisation. Visualisation is simple, effective, and long lasting. Visualisation is effective because you create an image of the desired result — to feel easier and more comfortable with people, to feel comfortable at meetings or in public speaking, to fit in better in your society, to improve your round of golf, to develop hobbies or other skills.

Visualisation is effective because you have full control over the desired outcome. You see yourself in your mind, giving a perfect business presentation. You see yourself talking to a small group of people, perhaps at work, or at a party. In your mind you can feel at ease. With perseverance, this is carried over to the real situation in the real world because the mind will, over time, accept these images you create as fact. The benefits are lasting.

In Your New Image

Visualisation is not new. It has been written about in academic books for many years—indeed decades. Individuals have tried it and benefited from it. It has been used, and is becoming more and more widely used, to coach sporting teams.

Clinical trials indicate that creative imagery gives truly amazing results if the person is sincere and persistent in wanting the desired result.

For decades, sports performance has been enhanced by this means. Golf and tennis and most other sports can be improved on a personal level by visualising that desired improvement.

Picture yourself playing golf next Sunday, and getting the best score you have ever attained. But do more than just think about that game. Imagine yourself—every free moment you have before next Sunday's game—lining up the ball, and taking the perfect swing at it. Yes, you could better your game significantly merely by picturing yourself playing. Does that sound too simple? Most people might think so, but it works. Creating images in your mind of what you want to achieve is about all there is to gaining the self-confidence to improve the way you do things in your life.

Tiger Woods does just that for his practice sessions—he sees himself hitting the ball perfectly every time he plays golf. Creative imagery is promoted more and more by sports psychologists to improve the performance of sportspersons, whether they are training in swimming, running, skiing, or any other sporting endeavour.

But let's not limit this technique to merely improving our performance in sports. Because our self-doubts are removed through this technique, we develop the self-confidence necessary to increase our levels of achievement in a wide range of activities and remove obstacles to reaching our goals.

Self-doubts are really a form of self-restriction. Being held back by what we know (or think we are able to achieve) is a cause of our stress and anxiety and disappointment. Creative imagery can give us the self-confidence to stand up to arrogant

Introduction

bosses, and to deal with difficult people. It can reduce the stress of shopping or attending meetings. It can help people who have a strong fear of flying, and those who suffer from agoraphobia or a fear of open spaces. In fact, it can be used effectively in treating those who suffer from any of the hundreds of phobias known to medicine.

Creative imagery is often used to boost self-confidence in dealing with threatening situations.

Self-doubt is possibly the single-most quoted factor by people who explain why they can't do something, or can't achieve what is expected of them. People use many different excuses that are, really, no more than limitations imposed by themselves (or imposed by others who have had an influence on that person's life). Their achievements end where they have erected that invisible barrier that tells them 'you are unable to pass through this point. Stop.'

And other activities, such as learning to drive a car, canoeing, rowing, welding to name just a few can be improved, merely by persistently picturing the desired outcome, practising, practising in the mind.

Clinical trials indicate that visualisation gives truly amazing results to anyone who is sincere and persistent in wanting those desired results.

My research over a number of years has shown more and more that visualisation can make big contributions to changing behaviour and attitudes without side effects, only benefits. It is inexpensive—indeed, there is no cost, other than finding the time necessary to do the required exercises. And it works!

This book shows you how to create the desired picture of what you want to achieve. It will discuss the merits of this safe, effective means to change behaviour and even improve sports performance and increase ability in any chosen hobbies, even study. It will show you how to relax, how to create and hold the images. It will discuss the expected improvement, and the limitations of the technique.

In Your New Image

In Your New Image takes you through every stage of relaxation, picturing the desired results, holding that image and achieving what you want. It will show you how you can remove doubts in your life and move on to important goals.

I expect there will be a number of readers who half-heartedly picture a change once or twice and say, 'I have got no benefit, it can't work.' It doesn't work that way. Throughout the book we will look at all the things they could be doing wrong. There is a fault-finding guide. It is likely you won't be holding the images for a long enough time, won't be serious in your attempts to attain the results you said you wanted, and simply can't be bothered with it after one or two sessions. To many, it will all seem oh so hard and futile. Perhaps these people need the book more than ever!

A number of ways to still achieve the desired results will be reinforced. I will emphasise being more persistent, creating a stronger image, perhaps changing the surroundings while performing the exercises, and changing your attitude to the whole technique. There will be a number of readers with a negative attitude. I will show these readers how to overcome their negative attitude through the same techniques so they can go on to achieve what they really thought they wanted to achieve in the first place.

There really is little reason why creative imagery will fail. All likely arguments and reasons and excuses are covered so the book covers the technique in the most effective way to remove self-doubts and their associated barriers to achievement.

The book will also look at the possible limitations of creative imaging. Despite its effectiveness, it still is not possible to achieve the impossible.

But what is the impossible? This word takes on different meanings for different people. For some, the impossible might be losing a few pounds of weight. That would be a negative attitude and one that can be easily overcome.

Introduction

To others, a paraplegic taking part in a race would be impossible. But look at the incredible results athletes have achieved at the Paralympic games! The impossible is truly a state of mind.

Is there a limit therefore as to what can be considered realistic? Perhaps not.

This book will show you how to create the desired picture of what you want to achieve. It discusses the merits of this safe, effective means to change your behaviour and your reaction to a number of common situations and even improve your sports performance and increase your ability in your chosen hobbies, even study. *In Your New Image* will show you how to relax, how to create and hold the images in your mind. It will discuss the expected improvement, and the limitations of visualisation.

In Your New Image covers aspects of how to achieve success in your life. The book uses a number of examples you will be able to relate to and see yourself in.

Success will come to you more and more rapidly, the more you practise the technique. From your first successes with this technique, you will most likely go on to achieve greater success and better performance in many aspects of your life.

I suggest you should look carefully at what you want to be and want to achieve and make sure your goals are what could be termed reasonable. But you are asked not to overlook the fact that what is not practical today can become very reasonable in the near future.

Would you like to become a winner? Would you like to have as much respect for yourself, for your abilities, as you would like others to have for you? I think it is quite unnecessary for anyone to answer those questions. We all would like to be winners, to succeed in whatever we undertake, to be successful in the full meaning of that term as it applies to us. Success is whatever we want it to be for ourselves. But I think it is safe to say that success is also to achieve what we aim for.

Believing in ourselves, being sure of ourselves, is what a new self-image is about. We see ourselves as successful. We become successful because of the way we see ourselves. We live the life that we continually imagine ourselves to lead. This, believe it or not, is just as important as improving our self-image so we no longer look at ourselves in the mirror each morning and squint at what we see.

My aim in writing this book was to share with as many people as possible the truly magnificent benefits that I and thousands of others have experienced with this easy, pleasurable, simple yet effective method of bringing about desired changes in our lives.

By creating the right positive images of ourselves, we can feel good about ourselves. The saying that it's all in the mind, although simplifying the result tremendously, is nevertheless true. When we see our image as positive and successful, then we will be just that. Unfortunately, not many of us see that image in the mirror as a truthful replica of our true selves. We see little blemishes that make us shy away from the real world. If, however, we look in that same mirror one morning and decide, yes, that is the image of a person who has personality, who commands respect, who is brim full with confidence, is talented, is going places, then that person will be all that.

And finally, what can you hope to achieve through the successful use of creative imagery? This might surprise you! It's almost anything you desire. It's anything you care to imagine.

I hope you will benefit as much as I have from visualisation and be able to achieve all that you set out to do.

Chapter 1 What's It All About?

It was the mid-1950s. My parents had just bought me a bicycle. It was old. It was heavy. It was a pale green, with a metallic sheen. I remember it well. I also remember that I couldn't ride it. For several weeks I didn't have the confidence to ride on my own. Instead, my brother would hold onto the seat (or at least I used to think he was holding onto me), so I wouldn't fall off. So much for the confidence of an eight year old child.

One day at school I was bored — a common experience with me in those years, as well as at frequent times during my teens and the earlier years of my adult life. But on that day at school I pictured myself on that green bicycle. I pictured myself sitting on the seat, leaning against the wall of the house, wanting to be able to ride. I had no anxiety about riding while all the activity was just in my mind. I remember pushing myself away from the wall (again in my mind) and riding down the driveway. I was riding — at least in my mind that was what I was doing.

I repeated this performance. It was painless — I didn't fall off, I didn't wobble any more than I should have, and I didn't hurt myself — perhaps my greatest fear at the time.

I repeated this performance over the next few days at school, and extended the trips beyond the gate and along the footpath. In my mind, I could ride. So I kept riding. I would turn corners, I could stop, I could do what any confident young cyclist of my age should have been able to do.

Several days later I got on the bicycle without thinking and rode down the driveway, opened the gate and rode along the footpath for some distance, although to a small child's mind, the trip seemed eternal.

Then I realised. There was no one behind me supporting me in case I fell off.

I had gained the confidence I needed to stay upright, to ride, and most important of all, to enjoy this activity.

Yet there was a crucial ingredient in all this that I didn't comprehend at the time and which only made sense many, many years later. It was that I had pictured myself performing this activity. I had succeeded in learning to ride my bicycle without practising!

USING CREATIVE IMAGERY TO IMPROVE PERFORMANCE

I wasn't aware at the time that experiments were taking place in America with baseball teams, in which one team would practise its hits all week, while the other team would imagine itself playing. The team that got the easy task was encouraged to sit back, find a comfortable, relaxed position, and merely imagine themselves hitting the ball, throwing the ball, responding to every likely move the opposition team could make. The results? There was no difference in the performance of either team!

SHARING THE EXPERIENCES

Without knowing the reason why it worked, I used the process of creating positive images in my mind a lot in later years. I had found something that had worked for me a couple of times, then a few more times, and then on even more occasions. I didn't know anything about psychology at the time, or about the workings of the mind. But things are a lot different now.

From those early times, I have used the same technique to learn how to weld metals, drive a car, feel confident giving a talk, and speaking to two hundred people. And I still use those

What's It All About?

same techniques to conduct meetings, to feel relaxed at taking examinations, to broadcast on radio, to feel comfortable in situations that, only a couple of weeks earlier would have been a nightmare. I used this technique to remove all doubts I had about my ability. These were all situations in which many, many people feel uncomfortable, ill at ease, even threatened. I learned how to control anxiety levels when my bosses had something to say to me — not always bad things, but early in my working life, they were threatening situations to me anyway.

Over the years I have been able to share these experiences with other people to overcome many of their fears, their inadequacies, their self-doubts, and to remove the anguish and personal torment they were obliged to face in their daily lives. Now I want to share this technique with you.

This technique is simple. It can be applied almost anywhere. You can use the technique in almost any situation — to learn new skills, to change your behaviour, to move your life forward.

Just like the others who have benefited from this simple, extremely effective technique, it will help you achieve much of what you want to achieve with your life as far as being able to remove psychological limits and self-doubts are concerned.

And over the years, creative imagery has found its way into more and more self-help books, and books on psychology and mind control and self achievement. It is so effective, it has become a common feature of many of the books on alternative therapies — psychologists and medical people are realising the benefits of this practice to achieve what they themselves often fail to accomplish.

Many people who are introduced to this technique are put off because of its seeming simplicity. It's almost a matter of saying 'picture the changes you want ... and they will eventuate'. That, basically, is it, although oversimplifying it. I will show you in this book how to attain the level of visualization necessary to bring about the desired changes. You will be shown how to hold the images of what you want to change in your personality and to improve your skills. But most importantly, you will have to do all the work. Your success at the end of each program you embark on is entirely up to you. Many things, if they are within your capacity, are achievable. You will have to concentrate for a period, depending on the extent of change you want to bring about, the standard you wish to achieve, and the time available for you to bring about the desired change you are seeking. But the hard work that you will have to put into the technique is no more than vivid daydreaming. Is that really hard?

THE LIMITS OF CREATIVE IMAGERY

Creative imagery has the ability to enhance what you are capable of doing. But let us not be silly about this. Obviously, if you have one leg, no amount of visualisation is going to help you win the high jump in the Olympic Games. No amount of picturing yourself doing so is going to get you pole vaulting if you have seriously injured your back. What creative imagery does is to increase your natural ability to achieve what you would otherwise be able to achieve under the best possible circumstances. It basically removes all your reservations about what you can and can't do, so you move ahead in your life and get on with the serious side of living your life as it was intended.

You will only be able to achieve what is possible, you won't be able to achieve the impossible. Let me give you an example. If you are a male, perhaps in your forties, and are getting rather thin on top, there is nothing all the self-created pictures in the world can do to reverse that process. But what you can easily achieve with creative imagery is your self-acceptance of your situation—liking yourself the way you are, accepting yourself with thinning hair and that distinctive look. But picturing it is not going to grow the hair back again.

And suppose you, like most of us, suffer from a degree of vanity, and you find you desperately need to start wearing glasses for reading. No amount of creative imagery is going to

What's It All About?

correct your eyesight to the extent where you can ask the optometrist for a refund of the cost of spectacles. But with creative imagery you can accept yourself very easily wearing glasses for reading, seeing yourself wearing them in the office or at meetings, and accepting yourself wearing them with pride.

What I am advocating here is pursuing only what is achievable within the limits of the practical. If you do not possess tertiary qualifications, you are most unlikely to become a professor at a university. That clearly is not achievable. If you lack the required qualifications to practise as a doctor, it is unlikely (unless you are bold and ruthless and break the law) that you will practise medicine.

What I am suggesting in this chapter, though, is if you want to become a surveyor so that you can work outside rather than behind a desk, then you can certainly get the required qualifications to become a registered surveyor and establish your own business. And if you want to become a biologist and work with wildlife to the exclusion of all else, then there is little to stop you, apart from the university fees and finding the time to study. And in my reference to establishing your own business, if you are a cleaner, there is nothing to stop you from setting up your own cleaning contract company and succeeding admirably at that venture. If you enjoy working with wood, or with metal, there is little that is really going to stop you from achieving those goals, apart from your attitude — and a negative attitude towards those goals is something that you will easily overcome with creative imagery. Again, the results are brought about because in every case, you are able to remove any self-doubts you may have, and reverse your previous idea of your capabilities.

DETERMINE THE IMPROVEMENTS YOU WANT IN YOUR LIFE

I suggest you look carefully at what you want to be and want to achieve and make sure your goals are what could be termed reasonable. But don't overlook the fact that what is not practical today, can become very reasonable in the next few weeks, months or years.

In looking at any of these changes you want to bring about for the better in your life, look at the total time—not how long any of these things are going to take for you to achieve them, but how many more years you will have in your working life if you are not happy. If you are thirty and want to be a surveyor, the study might take five years to complete. You will still have thirty years left in the work force to enjoy your chosen career. And if you are fifty and want to work with wood, you will still have fifteen or twenty more years to enjoy this too. How long will you have left in the work force doing what you are doing now? Yes, about the same time. So what is the preferred option? A bit of sacrifice now is worth many, many years of satisfaction and enjoyment in the future.

So from now, whenever I mention surging ahead in your life, look at the practicalities of what you want to achieve, looking first at the background that is going to lead you to where you want to go.

Employers are not looking only for the right skills when recruiting staff. They are also looking for the way applicants can speak clearly and with confidence. This too is achievable with creative imagery, because you will be able to remove your doubts about your ability to give dynamic presentations at work. I'll show you later on how to do that. Employers are looking for the way applicants can interact with other staff. Even if at present you are the shyest and most nervous individual on earth, creating positive images of yourself performing a particular task is going to help you considerably

What's It All About?

to overcome what you might see as a handicap to promotion. Or a handicap to anything else you want to achieve.

Most people fail an interview an hour before they start talking to the interviewers. They get themselves into such a state of failure that they predict their own outcome. They picture themselves performing badly, answering straightforward questions by stammering out of control. It is not surprising they perform badly. This is not because they do not know their subject—indeed, many applicants, if they were to answer the same questions in general conversation, would be seen to be extremely knowledgeable. But, because of how they see themselves at that important interview, the results are dismal. They have, in all probability, rehearsed the worst outcome in their minds, for days. With positive pictures of your desired outcome, this whole result and performance can be turned around so that you perform much better.

Creative imagery will be able to help you in circumstances such as if you now feel uncomfortable with the opposite sex — with the guidance you will receive in this book, you will be able to overcome your shyness. Shyness is, surprisingly, quite widespread, but it need not be. With the creative imagery techniques outlined in this book, that too could soon be a thing of the past. Remove your self-doubts, and a whole new world is waiting for you. You will feel confident in public speaking or in attending meetings. You will be able to put all fears and tension in these activities in the past. You will be able to feel comfortable with your colleagues at work. You will be able to use the techniques of creating positive images to acquire new skills, and to enhance your expertise in sports such as golf, or ball games.

Bringing about most changes is not beyond the expectations of this proven method. I will work with you, and show you how to bring about the desired results in your own life, because later in this book I have included exercises that you will be able to identify with, covering a number of improvements that you may wish to achieve in your life. Losing that anxiety before you attend that important job interview, removing the jitters and nervousness before you sit for that final examination are just some of the examples I have included. If you now lack confidence, creating the right mental pictures will help you overcome that and build up your self-esteem so that you feel comfortable talking and mixing with people.

I don't mean that the improvements will be slight. If you practise the exercises properly and adequately as outlined in this book, you will achieve all you set out to gain, and possibly to a much higher degree than you could ever have expected. And creative imagery benefits do not stop there. The technique has helped many people overcome fear of travel, fear of train travel, fear of boating, of animals, dogs, spiders, and a fear of open spaces (agoraphobia).

This book goes one step further in helping you to easily attain what you want.

Let me give you a word of warning though. Whatever you set out to achieve, don't overdo things. Don't aim at being so 'perfect' that you become unpopular. While I will be the first to admit that, through the principles described in this book you will be able to achieve great changes in your life, I certainly do not want to see you go to the other end of the scale and remove all that is human about you.

FORGET THE PAST

Not all personal problems, fears and reactions stem from incidents in childhood, no matter how traumatic these might seem now, or might have seemed at the time. There is considerable conflicting opinion on this subject. That is why creative imagery stands out on its own. It deals with you as you are at this very moment—not with you as you were thirty years ago. It deals with how you feel, how you regard others, how you regard yourself right now.

What's It All About?

Many other therapies call for regression—a most painful experience for most people. Because creative imagery is very effective in dealing with the present (and this carries well into the future as well), there is no need to look at your past. Why relive what your subconscious mind has found so awful that it wants to forget? Whatever has happened, happened long ago. Those incidents, individually or collectively, might or might not have affected your moods, your behaviour and attitudes of today. But it's the future that is ahead of you and, treated right, the future can be a very inviting place for you to be in. It can be full of promises, promises of a far better life for you and your loved ones.

Coming to grips with your childhood will not make your adult problems go away. Reliving your past won't make you feel any better about yourself. There is quite a lot of evidence available now to suggest that this type of therapy does not work, is not long lasting, and often digs up bitterness and resentment that in itself causes further problems for the individual.

Just like the mind can block out traumatic events of our lives so that we barely recall them except perhaps under the influence of hypnosis, failure to visualise clearly may be a blocking action that our minds set up as a defence against what we might see of ourselves. Unfortunately, unless you come to accept whatever it is that is holding you back now, you will not be able to move forward. With creative imagery, it is not necessary to recreate any traumatic events in your mind. In fact, with creative imagery, it is certainly quite unnecessary to relive any such events at all. It is sufficient merely to see yourself in your current situation—how you feel, how you react to all that is around you now. It is unnecessary to go back in your life beyond the present. What makes you shy away from tall men might be behaviour that stemmed from an incident with your father, uncle, or even a stranger. You now react in a certain way, although the original incident might well be forgotten by now.

Leave it forgotten. With creative imagery, it is sufficient to picture your reaction now — at this moment — to certain circumstances. And you know how you react, so there is no reason to delve into your past, and nothing to 'dig up' that can traumatise you.

BELIEF IS THE SECRET

Placebos can be as effective as morphine is as a painkiller in over seventy percent of trials. The recipients believe they are receiving morphine, so the patients expect to get relief from serious pain, therefore the placebo works. This is the strength and the power of belief. And with creative imagery, you make your mind believe the images you create, therefore they become fact. Affirmations — the process of simply repeating words — seldom work. The mind needs to convert words into images before it can act on them. Affirmations may help a little if used in conjunction with the pictures you will create, but I don't think they are going to bring about all the results that you can achieve with positive images.

Most people take the easy solution, and if you are one of the majority, then you will have no difficulty mastering the techniques for success outlined in this book, because there is nothing hard about sitting down and visualising and daydreaming about 'what could be', because what you picture in your mind — as long as you picture it strongly enough, and often enough, can very soon become 'what is'.

SEE WHAT YOU WANT

To bring about the desired results with creative imagery, it is necessary to imagine the changes you want, as if they have already occurred, so you would see yourself in the situation of change you sought. You see yourself feeling at ease with and facing the large-figured boss so he is no longer threatening to you. You would see yourself sitting in the dentist's chair as if

What's It All About?

nothing too bad is going to happen to you. You see the result that you want. The successful athlete imagines the joy of victory even before he begins to run, sees himself crossing the finishing line ahead of the other competitors even before he knows what day the race is on. He sees victory. He feels it. He experiences it. So will you when you remove all those reservations and self-doubts in your mind.

The successful sales person pictures the customer buying as he makes his presentation. The salesperson sees that client becoming interested, sees that person handing over the money, signing the contract, or whatever is involved in closing a particular sale. Successful selling is seeing the salesperson with the client and the end result and, this is very important, feeling the joy of closing a difficult sale, feeling just what it is like to achieve this end result. Are you in sales? Think of what this will mean for you in your work.

The successful writer pictures writing books or magazine articles, and sees people eagerly reading whatever he has written. The successful author pictures his book in a bookstore window as he writes the manuscript.

These people do more than picture these events. They live them, feel the emotion of winning, hear the sounds around them in their environment as they reach their goal. They live this image constantly.

So what is victory? It is easy to see how a salesperson can become successful by creating all the scenes he will face in making his presentations to his customers. We can image how an athlete must visualise winning. But how do we change? How do we achieve success? By picturing success!

Let's take the mystery out of creative imagery. In fact, there is no mystery. Harry Emerson Fosdick wrote, 'hold a picture long and steady enough in your mind's eye and you will be drawn towards it ... Great living starts with a picture held in your imagination of what you would like to do or be.' This is the secret of creative imagery. What would you like to achieve in your life?

You have to think success before you can experience it. Visualisation is a powerful tool for achieving that. The foundations of all achievement are almost always formed in great visions — visions of the self, visions of the future, visions of success.

VISIONS OF SUCCESS

But let us define success. Success is very personal. To me it is having my freedom to be myself, to be creative, using self-expression. To others, success might be getting rapid promotions in their careers. Others might see success as having lots of money, a successful home life and happy family. For each of us, these are all equally important to be termed successes. It is us, and only ourselves as individuals, who must determine priorities that suit ourselves. And it is essential not to be influenced by other people's reasoning in determining our own success. You will not feel happy in yourself if you are trying to match your personality, your interests to other people's classification of 'success'. It's the same as if you asked someone what sort of job you should do when you leave school, and were told what that person would like to be. Basing your life on someone else's definition of success is going to make you just as miserable as going into a career that is quite wrong for you. Taking advice from others as to what the definition of success should mean to you is just as foolish. Don't take advice in this area. Never!

So whenever I refer to success in this book, I mean that goal that you see, that you have set for yourself, and no one else.

Let me give you another word of warning. Sometimes, because of the unintended misleading advice that is too frequently given out, it is wise not to disclose your immediate plans or goals to others, unless you are absolutely sure that any

What's It All About?

advice will be given without bias, and is reliable and is appropriate to you. Much good-intentioned advice about success, or whatever, is worse than useless if it is not based on your personal goals.

Within reason, you have control over your present and your future, and I am being very liberal by saying that you have control within reason. There will be some things happening to us from time to time that will be beyond our control. But we have no control over our past. That's happened. We can't change anything that has happened to us up to this very moment. We can't change what happened to us this morning, or last weekend, or when we were ten years old. But from this moment forward, that is different. With confidence, we can take control of our lives and alter our possible fate for the better, and make our future a nice place to spend the rest of our lives.

FEEL SECURE IN THE FUTURE

Throughout the book I am advocating change. Change in ourselves, changes in our attitudes, changes in what awaits us. But to many, change is threatening. It represents a venture from the known to the uncertainty of the unknown. To many people, sameness is their security. They feel happy if nothing around them changes.

Many people forget that the known, the 'now' of our lives can be full of risks too. There is little in the way of job security these days. How will you cope with that change if it is forced upon you? Will you shrivel, disintegrate, feel your life has come to an abrupt end? There is little security in relationships, or even marriage any more. How will you cope if yours comes to an abrupt end? Or will you face imposed change with confidence? Would you have sufficient courage and confidence to go on and start anew if you were amongst the statistics of relationship breakdowns? It's a big, changing world out there, with changes coming about faster than they have in any previous time of humanity.

Creative imagery is a means of unblocking the barriers we ourselves have created, and a means of removing our self-doubts. Creative imagery can lead to a new way of living, in which we are able to accept everything that is thrown at us. Creating positive mental images can build us up so that the worst is not so bad after all, and so we have something to start with all over again when the dust has settled on the calamity that we have just gone through, or are about to go through.

If you really believe that you could never become the person you want to be, it's time to change your image of yourself. Our self-image is the key to our personality. Because of this, our experiences verify, and thereby strengthen, our self-image. Self-fulfilling prophecies could never be stronger. You need confidence and it is obvious that you do not have it if you believe in failure.

SEE YOURSELF FOR REAL
You will act like the sort of person you think you are. If you think yourself not very bright, you won't be. If you think yourself unlucky, you will not be lucky. If you think yourself timid, a poor speaker and poor at interviews and dismal at examinations, so be it. But think differently, picture yourself not as you see yourself now, but as you would like to be, confident, a good speaker, successful, a person with whatever you have identified as appealing to your personality and your interests and lifestyle, then this could also be you. Just picture it for a moment. Picture yourself as ... well, what is it that you would like to become?

What's It All About?

SEEING THE POSSIBLE

Don't limit yourself. There are already far too many individuals with self-imposed limitations who continue to fail to reach their full potential.

You will not be successful by this time tomorrow. That's because the mind needs sufficient time to accept the images you create as if they are real events. But from several weeks — usually about three weeks or four — after really giving the techniques in this book your best attention and concentrating on the imaging as if it is the only thing that matters, then you will at least be on your way to wherever you are going. But ... don't give up after only one day. You will remain right where you are now. Tomorrow will be the same as today was, and next year will be mighty similar to what this year has been for you so far.

Few of us have the vision to realise what is possible. Many of us restrict ourselves by what we think, and what others think, we can or should do. By creating positive pictures in your mind of where you want to go, you will be off to a very good start. But you must have an open mind that the desired changes are possible. A closed mind won't help you here. If you believe imaging won't help, you will never get the right mood, the right feel, your emotions will only be overcrowded by negative thoughts and images that will defeat the whole program even before you get started. But why have that attitude?

Obviously there is much more to achieving a goal than imagining success once or twice. However, you have to think success before you can experience it and creative imagery is a powerful tool to that end. You often need follow-up in the way of actual performance. Just as you can finish a trade course and know the basics involved to get you started, you need hands-on experience to make your touch professional, no matter what your vocation. So too creative imagery must be followed up by practice in the real world. But that, by then, is easy! Any skill, any activity, becomes easier with lots of rehearsing and practice. Any skill needs constant doing.

HEAD IN THE RIGHT DIRECTION

Just as the seeds of great achievement are almost always sown in a great vision, once you picture your goals, once you get a taste of them, you live them, you dream them, they are part of you and your thoughts. That enthusiasm, that excitement alone is often enough to drive you on towards your aim, and assist you in achieving whatever it is you want.

As with any destiny, it is essential to decide where you are going, what you want, and know what it takes to get you there. Picture whatever it is that you want in your life so clearly that the images you create of the changes you want and the success you want, become reality.

Many, many people dream of winning a large sum in a lottery. The chances of that are very, very small indeed. The odds are far higher in achieving success in your own right. The self-satisfaction and the glory of doing things that way, your way, are much higher than merely being able to say, 'I won it. Wasn't I lucky?' It is far better to say, 'I did it my way. Aren't I a true success?'

Think of where you could be. And the funny thing about that statement is that just about everyone who reads this book will, if they apply the principles in this book sincerely and for a very reasonable time, move that most difficult mountain of all — themselves.

FREEDOM FOR ALL

Creative imagery is a means of unlocking the gates we ourselves have closed. Creative imagery can reward us with our freedom.

What is freedom? For me, it means one thing. For you, possibly something quite different. So freedom is, in many ways, like success — it's personal. Freedom may be a lifestyle. It may be choosing the job that you want rather than the one you now have. Freedom might be the means to change career direction and move to a new area of your life. Freedom may mean having the courage to cut your ties and move to a new location that you would find challenging and stimulating, interesting and rewarding, rather than the one you have now, which might be a cultural desert.

Freedom is not having someone looking over your shoulder to see what you are doing. It means moving ahead, beyond that, beyond the routine of a mundane job where you are just a small cog. Quite often freedom is restricted because it is tied to your feeling of insecurity and self-doubt. If you feel secure in yourself, confident, feel that you can competently handle much more than you do now, then your freedom's boundaries are extended dramatically.

Freedom might even be not having to work with the people you don't like. Freedom is moving beyond other people's little worlds. Freedom is moving beyond your little world, your little circle. Freedom is having the courage to get out of where you are and getting to where you want to be.

How can you achieve that? Through confidence, by changing your self-image, by changing the way you do things, the way you see yourself, by changing your attitudes towards yourself, changing your attitudes towards other people.

Freedom is not having to put up with the nonsense, the irrelevancies, the trivia of your work situation and your social environment, but instead having the confidence you can develop through creative imagery to move to another world, to a world that is meaningful, challenging, demanding, rewarding, the world that is there waiting to be taken.

Too many of us are locked into our mundane situations through lack of courage, lack of seeing ourselves in new roles, the roles we would really like to be in.

Freedom is a hundred things. It is a hundred things to a hundred people. Freedom is not something you crave for while you are in prison, or in political exile, or restrained by political powers. Freedom is the ability to do what you want. You can achieve your freedom through creative imagery.

People start wars for freedom. There are campaigns to free people, from prison, from political asylum. Why aren't you freeing yourself from your asylum?

Freedom is creativity. Freedom is self-expression. Freedom is saying in your own way, in your own voice, verbally or in writing, what you as an individual think. With confidence, and a good self-image, you can be as free as you want. Freedom is ridding yourself of the ties to the things you don't like. Freedom is independence, independence from the things you don't want in your life. Applying the principles in this book, seeing yourself in a new role in each of these situations is easily and painlessly attainable.

Freedom is doing what you believed you couldn't previously do, attaining for you what was the impossible just a short time ago. It is doing something openly and enjoying it.

You may be locked into a small job now, be a small person in a small world, with people looking over your shoulder. You may right now feel timid, you may feel that people are checking up on your work. Possibly they are. Move beyond that.

Improve your education, your skills, your training. Improve a lot of things.

This book will show you how you can.

It won't show you how to learn a whole lot more, nor how to learn a particular field, but it will show you how to improve your study methods. It will show you how to prepare yourself for examinations, prepare yourself for what's ahead of you. I mean all the good things. I mean the real future. That is where you are going to spend the rest of your life. If you get it right now, it will be worth it, won't it?

If you tie up a horse, it won't go far. It won't go fast. If you remove those shackles from the animal, it will go fast. If you remove those shackles from your mind, you will be like that horse that gallops to where it wants to go. The animal will find its own freedom, and there will be no stopping it, no holding it back. If you unshackle your mind from all the things that have

What's It All About?

restrained you up to now — your self-doubts, your poor self-image — imagine what you could be if you were free to do anything you wanted to do, could achieve anything you wanted to achieve. Imagine what your life would be today. Was your day challenging today? Possibly it was. Could you have done a lot more though, perhaps in a different field of work?

Were you completely satisfied with what you achieved today? Maybe you were. If not, what could you have done? What would you have preferred to have done today? Would you rather have worked for yourself? This book will give you the confidence to do just that. You will believe you really can be a success in your own business. Would you rather have taken up some stimulating study? Creative imagery will show you how you can. Perhaps started a new course? Taken up a new hobby? Perhaps you felt you lacked the ability to study. Creative imagery will instil in you the confidence you will need for that direction in your life.

LOOK AHEAD

Over the next few weeks you could remove many of those barriers so you don't have too many more days like you had today.

Is tomorrow going to be better for you? Maybe. Is tomorrow going to be one of those days in which you are going to have the boss looking over your shoulder again? Is tomorrow going to be a day when you go to work, do your routine job and go home? Surely there's more in life than that for you. Surely you want more from life than that.

Over the next few days, or weeks, take your time and decide what freedom is to you. Look at the barriers. Look at the shackles that prevent you from going from what you are now, where you are now, to what you would like to be, where you would like to be.

In Your New Image

So what is holding you back? You'll find the answers further along in this book. Look back over today. What held you back? What made your job, your life, ordinary? Draw a chart of two columns, one of them for where you are now and to include what you are doing now, and the other showing where you would like to be and what you would like to be doing in the future. This chart should cover all aspects of your life — work, personal, hobbies, skills — list all the things you can think of that are important to you, even the seemingly little things. You might like to improve your work situation. What would this require of you? Does this involve talking at meetings? Does it require that you give presentations at work? Does it include holding and chairing meetings? Does it mean playing social games of golf with your clients? Do you feel uneasy about this? Would you like to move out of administration and into sales? Into public relations or advertising? Would you like to move into another whole new area of your work, perhaps embark on a new career? A new place of employment perhaps, one that is not so stifling? List everything that you would like to achieve, everything you would like to be doing. Don't regard anything as too small, too unimportant, to include here. Never regard this list as closed. If well into the future you can identify some aspect of your life that does not please you, list it and do something about it!

Hobbies — would you like to take up carpentry? Metalwork? Would you like to take up home electronics? Would you like to take up needlework, or sewing? Quilt making or cross stitching? Would you like to take up repairing old cars? Restoring furniture? Do you feel you lack the confidence to do this now? Would you like to learn to weld and build a yacht, or to build something out of wood — a table, ornate chairs, or a bookcase? Would you like to improve your golf, or to take up tennis and be good at it? Do you wish you could write books for children, write poetry, or write technical works for which you may well have a suitable background?

What's It All About?

If you lack the confidence to do these things, imagine what you could achieve if you had that necessary confidence. Imagine the difference your life would be if you could do each and every one of those skills that you desire. This is why preparing that list is so important — to help you focus on what you want from life.

PICTURE A PERFECT DAY

Sit back, relax, and imagine the perfect day. What would you do on that perfect day? Oh, yes, I know, a lot of you would say, 'lie on the beach for twenty-four hours'. Realistically, list every aspect of what you see on your perfect day. Don't worry about night time, don't worry about the sun going down. Imagine twenty-four hours of bright sunlight. Divide it — eight hours work, eight hours recreation, eight hours family. What would you be doing if tomorrow were that perfect day of twenty-four hours?

There's a blue sky, it's warm, sunny. For eight hours, would you learn skiing? Would you improve your round of golf? Would you learn to hit the ball properly, use the right clubs? And in your eight hours of work, would you like to make those eight hours full of challenge, full of satisfaction? Of course you would.

What does that require? What skills would you have to learn and develop?

Imagine being able to go home after work and say to your family, 'I had a fantastic day. I did this, I did that. Gee, I feel good. That was a perfect work day. There isn't another thing I would have liked to have done. I gave a talk to the managers, and that was well received by the whole audience. I met three big clients, I made two sales. My boss congratulated me on the way I approached my clients, on the way I closed those sales. He has asked me to talk to the other sales people tomorrow and motivate them so they can learn from my experience.' Were you able to say that when you got home this evening? Yesterday evening? Does all this sound far-fetched? No, it's not. Not at all. Many, many others before you have made similar transformations in their lives, and achieved remarkable feats like these. Let me work with you for a few weeks so you can start to achieve transformations like these yourself. That's all it takes — a few weeks.

Imagine the recreational side of that perfect day of yours. Would you like to work at a new hobby? Develop your existing hobby and improve your skills at it? Wouldn't it have been nice to have taken your family away for a day's skiing?

Imagine being with your family — you are calm, relaxed, loving, appreciative of what they do.

If you are serious about attaining that perfect day, every day, stick at it. Change the things you don't like, remove those shackles, remove those barriers to getting ahead. Earn your freedom!

So how sincere are you? For some of you, and I hope there are not many like this, you would feel more secure doing the mundane, going off to work on Monday, doing your little bit, going home. That to you might be security. You're happy. You don't want change.

If that to you is what life is all about, then this book is going to be of little value.

However, if you go off to work on Monday at nine o'clock and want to change your lot, improve your outlook, but feel you need a push in the right direction, then we will work together to steer you to where you want to go. Things can, and will, move.

NEVER GIVE UP

While you are developing yourself and your skills, be patient. It may mean putting up with mundaneness for a little bit longer, it might mean putting up with people looking over your shoulder for a bit longer. It might mean nothing changes in your work life, in your home life for a little while. Develop your skills and then look for the possible moves in your life. Develop the skills to give you the opportunity to change your work situation so people don't look over your shoulder, so they don't give you trivial, meaningless tasks to do. You will know your capabilities once you start working on these exercises. By the time you have worked through this book, done the visual exercises, you probably will never use the words 'shortcoming', 'deficiency', 'limit' again in your life as far as they apply to you.

There are, of course, limitations. You may change and get in your mind what is, for you, the perfect home life. If your partner does not believe in this, or share your enthusiasm for the changes you want to bring about in your life, and if your partner is happy with things as they are, then there is, unfortunately, little more you can do in the immediate future.

Make sure your expectations are realistic. You may say I will give this new approach to my work a fair go. In three, six, ten weeks you may be full of confidence, you may have developed the ability to give presentations at work, to talk with confidence to your business associates. You may have developed skills you never thought you could acquire. But be realistic.

If the opportunity is there, you will be equipped to go for it. But because you are equipped for them, it does not mean that you will get every opportunity you want—at least not immediately. And at work, your department, your firm, your boss, may not have the opportunities for you to move ahead. Despite your personal achievements, you boss might be one of those who likes to put down their staff—and in a warped way, derive pleasure from such actions. You may want to get into sales. Your firm may not have an area such as a sales, or advertising, department.

Don't let that stop you from developing your skills, developing what you really want. Then when the opportunity comes up, you will be able to move into the right area, perhaps in another firm. Despite the immediate lack of opportunity, you are far better off and better equipped than you were three months ago. You have those skills to move on when the opportunities arise—you can now go for them.

You have seen an advertisement in the newspaper for a position. Three months ago you might have decided that it was not you the firm was looking for. You can look at the advertisement now and say 'that's me, that sounds like a beaut job. That sounds just like the one that I want. That's what I have in mind. It sounds challenging, it sounds good. Think I'll go for it'. You have the personal attributes the firm is looking for. You are a very good speaker. You are dynamic, self-assured. That's the type of person they are looking for in this position. Go on, go for it! You may not get it, but you now have a good chance. You probably are the person they are looking for. Be patient. Now that you have got to this stage, what's ahead of you is just finding that position. It's just finding that niche.

Hang in there a little bit longer, be choosy, pick the positions you really want. Don't be meek any more and say that, although you want a change, this one is the same as the one I am doing, so I think I'll give it a go. With change, the opportunity will soon follow, and everything else will fall into place. Maybe soon, maybe a little time down the track.

THERE ARE NO LIMITS TO WHAT IS ACHIEVABLE

These are the things you can overcome with creative imagery. If you are starting right from the back, work on it. You might feel you are overweight, you don't accept yourself because you are short, or too tall, or your speech might not be the best, you may stammer a little. Okay, start accepting yourself as you are. Then move on and improve the way you speak, then accept your weight, or hair loss. You will begin to like yourself. You will attain the social qualities, the traits that you want that are going to make you feel better.

What's It All About?

It isn't always helpful to see yourself as others see you, or even the way you think others see you ... They have different standards for judging people, different agendas, different defeating mechanisms. It is important to see yourself for yourself, and form a self-image based on experiences that are satisfying and on the images I will show you how to create in the rest of this book. Be an individual. Be yourself. Don't be the way someone else would have liked to have created you. You may realise that that hasn't worked. Well, now is the time to let go of the old traditions, the way you saw yourself, the way you see the world, and look at yourself and the world through good, clean glasses.

Don't conform any more than you really need to. Yes, you will have to be punctual if you want to keep your job. And yes, you will have to leave home at a certain time each morning if you wish to catch the train or bus. But within our everyday lives, there is a lot of scope still for individualism. If you like to laugh, laugh. If you like to tell a joke, tell it.

PREPARE YOURSELF FOR CHANGES
If you think you can do something, do it. If you think someone else could do it but doubt whether you could, then through creative imagery—creating positive images of yourself having achieved just that—you too will be able to accomplish it. Remember, it is you who is placing those limits on yourself now, no one else. Not your parents any more. Not your boss. Not your brothers or sisters any more. They did have a tremendous influence once over your thinking, your reactions to numerous situations. But now they are in the past, their influence is in the past. You are on your own. Now, let's get on with getting everything we possibly can out of life. Can you cope with that much change? At first, most people say 'no, let's ... leave things ... just as they are'. But let's do things slowly, one thing at a time, so we can grasp the changes as single issues.

Together, all the changes you can induce could accumulate to a tremendous wealth of possibilities and opportunities.

But what does it take ... all this change? Probably not much more than a fresh look at yourself. I am serious. Through the exercises described in this book, and a consideration of individual situations that many of us confront, or have confronted in our everyday lives, you can turn the past around, and from now on develop a fresh life for yourself. The one that you want. The one that you have often admired in other people.

Through this book, I am going to show you how to achieve success, and change your life for the better. I will work with you to remove your self-doubts and build your level of confidence. Together we will take that fresh look at yourself, so you like what you see, and can look towards a bright, happy and prosperous future. You are going to move on that path leading to the new you.

Chapter 2 How It Works

Stammering. Nervousness. Shyness. Fear of public speaking. Uneasiness with the opposite sex.

How did we get to be like that?

You may be familiar with the term conditioning. If you are, you will recall the experiments Ivan Pavlov, a Russian physiologist, whose main line of research was the physiology of digestion, performed on dogs. Typically, several times a bell would be rung just before the dogs were fed, and the animals salivated on receiving the food. Then the bell would be rung without the presentation of food. Pavlov noticed that the dogs salivated merely in response to the bell's ringing. Pavlov discovered that salivation could also be induced in dogs by the sight of the food container, even before they were fed, or by the presence of the attendant who normally fed the animals.

The result is what has become known as a conditional reflex. The conditional reflex is a nervous reflex. If an animal, however, conditioned in one way is moved to a new environment, it loses its original conditional reflex.

Although nearly all Pavlov's work was performed on dogs, similar responses have been shown to occur in mice and primates. Although the term 'conditional response' is more correct, it has, through the decades of use since Pavlov's research days, become known simply as conditioning.

Humans, like Pavlov's dogs, are easily conditioned. Conditioning in humans can begin at an early age—often in early childhood, but will continue right through life. With humans, it works like this. Suppose we are doing something as a child, and our parents remind us constantly, 'Don't do that, you will fall and hurt yourself.' Over time (and not all that long a time period is required for conditioning to make itself felt in our minds), we really believe that we are going to fall and get hurt. We develop a fear of whatever it was that we were trying to do to enjoy ourselves. It leaves us with a very nasty taste. So for the rest of our lives, unless measures are taken to overcome this fear, we will go through life with the constant fear associated with that particular activity.

Sometimes with conditioning, there needs to be only an association with an object at the time the person adversely reacted to a certain incident or event. The object, then, triggers the conditional response.

WHAT IF ... WHAT DOES IT MATTER?

Unfortunately, our society is almost governed by the thought — what if? I won't do this because what if? I shouldn't try that, because what if? I should watch out, because I never know what if!

What if. It affects all of us to some degree. We all limit ourselves, restrict our enjoyment, limit our capabilities, because what if that unknown should happen. Often we do not know what that 'what if' aspect might be, but we react as if something serious is going to happen nevertheless.

We don't go rock fishing because a freak wave might wash us off the rocks. We don't go bushwalking or tramping, because a snake might bite us. We don't go swimming, because a shark might take us. We don't go to parties anymore because we don't know who might be there.

Consequently, with a lifetime of what-ifs and similar acts of conditioning behind us, we really are restricted in our true capabilities. Most of us live with our conditioning, and are governed by it. But it is rather interesting that people who defy these warnings seldom suffer the fate that was predicted for their actions.

I am not suggesting that we should all go out and not take reasonable precautions. I am suggesting that, over our lifetimes, other people's good intentions about our health and safety often have a negative effect on our lives. Yes, we could be taken by a shark. But it does not happen very often. Yes, we could break our leg bushwalking or tramping. But that does not happen very often. We could step on a snake and suffer from its venom. But snake bites in developed countries are rather rare, considering the number of people who encounter snakes without harm overtaking them.

Consequently, through this conditioning, not many of us know how to really have fun, live life to the fullest, getting everything we can out of every moment of every day.

Creative imagery can reverse just about any of the effects of conditioning that have built up over perhaps even a lifetime.

We might also become conditioned to an outcome by actual experience—not merely being told something might happen. We might step on a snake and feel very frightened indeed. We are left with the memory of how we felt, our rapidly declining strength as the venom took effect. We would have that feeling, that memory with us for a long time, and this possibly would help us decide to restrict our tramping activities in snake-infested areas, at least for a while.

We might meet a large shark face to face one day while we are swimming or snorkelling That would deter most of us from going into the water for a long time afterwards, if ever again.

These events could be real, but they are very, very infrequent. It is a sad waste of a major part of our lives not to experience the enjoyment of an activity merely because something like this might happen. What about all the times when such events won't occur, didn't happen, and possibly will never occur? There is a difference between a real threat and being told that something might befall us.

It is also important to realise that we all react to different situations in quite different ways. A person can see a snake and merely walk around it, while others will give up walking forever. And there is the full range of reactions between those two extremes.

It is likely that the person who has seen numerous snakes will be the one who merely walks around the reptile, knowing it won't cause any deliberate harm or inflict a bite unnecessarily.

OUR CHILDHOOD IS STILL WITH US

You might, as a small child, have been nervous, and when you first began to speak, someone made a comment or two to the effect that you were a poor talker. You heard the remark, and were reluctant to say much to anyone any more. The result is that this single event has been holding you back right through to your adulthood.

One simple event, one innocent remark could have brought about that life-long change in your development and in your personality. Instead of being outgoing like other children, you possibly were always in fear of what someone might say each time you spoke. The result is not only the life-long fear you have experienced in even trying to hold a general conversation, but that constant fear that you might still hold, after forty or fifty years, that you are going to say the wrong thing at the wrong time. The original incident has long since passed—quite possibly, you can't even remember it now. You think you have moved on, but you haven't. You are still influenced by that feeling of nervousness. How much more enriched would your life have been had you not heard that remark, but instead got on with your life like all the other kids you grew up with?

There are numerous experiences that are part of growing up. We all react differently to each and every one of them. How each one affects us at the time determines, to a large degree, how we react to similar situations in the future.

But this does not necessarily need to be so. Just as Pavlov discovered that the conditional response can be changed in dogs, rats and primates, so too can it be changed in ourselves.

There is a bright world out there. You will want to be a part of it, leading a fulfilled life full of experiences, adventure, learning and pleasures.

OVERCOMING THE CONDITIONING

By using creative imagery as I will outline for you later in this book, you will learn how you can overcome those barriers and reverse much of that conditioning that has held you back from achieving a lot more than you already have.

How does creative imagery work?

The brain visualises pictures rather than uses words. We communicate with each other through the use of words, but these words consciously or not are transferred as images in our mind.

Scientific research has shown that when we visualise carrying out a specific activity, we alter our brain programs as if we were actively performing that activity. There are electro-chemical changes in the cells which produce new behaviour. So when we picture ourselves performing some feat, our brain acts and responds as if we are actually doing what we are picturing. To the brain, there is no difference between doing and picturing the activity. And in reality you will find that, when you have developed the techniques of creative imagery, there are no real differences between the two activities.

GET A PICTURE OF LIFE

Mentally rehearse whatever it is that you want to achieve. Only you should decide what it is that you want from your life. Don't

In Your New Image

leave that choice up to anyone else. Then go on to create and develop the mental pictures of that change you want to bring about in your life. There could be many such changes. Work on them one after the other with creative imagery. Your mind will eventually accept those images that you have created long enough as the 'real thing' and act according to how real they seem to it.

Creative imagery is the technique of using your imagination to create what you want in your life. There is nothing at all new, strange or unusual about it. You are already using it every day. The techniques expressed throughout this book are merely an extension of what you can already do, but by focusing on a desired result, the possibilities are enormous. Quite likely you have used creative imagery to picture yourself feeling very nervous at the examination you will be sitting for in the next week or so.

Or you might at present be picturing that important job interview that is going to change your career, that you want so much right now. Instead of focusing on a relaxed scene in the interview room, giving sensible, well thought out responses to the questions, you are quite possibly picturing all the things that will go wrong, all the silly things you will say, and what a fool you will make of yourself at the interview. This much I can predict with a high degree of accuracy. If this describes you, then I am sure that you will say stupid things to the interviewers. I am sure that you will make a complete fool of yourself, even though you know the field of work very well and are competent to handle the responsibilities more than adequately. And I predict with a high degree of certainty that you will talk too fast. My last prediction is that you won't get that job you want so much.

How am I so sure of this, for someone that I haven't yet met?

It's easy. You are predicting the outcome, picturing it, rehearsing it, picturing every silly answer you are going to give. You are picturing yourself being a blob of jelly in front of the people who are giving this important interview, giving you a splendid opportunity to better yourself. You will be like that, because you have pictured it so clearly so many times. Your mind has accepted that that is you, and will ensure that you react accordingly at the right time. Unfortunately for you, it is quite the wrong time.

THINK DIFFERENTLY ... ACT DIFFERENTLY

Think how different that interview could be if you changed the set of pictures, and instead, pictured yourself (perhaps over a couple of weeks, or at least as long as you have since you were asked to attend the interview), sitting in the interview room, relaxed, looking at the interviewers as you answer the questions in a slow, confident voice and style. If you had pictured yourself with so much confidence, your future could be heading in a different direction. Instead, where will you be working next week? Probably in the same office, at the same desk.

So the sooner you realise that visualising the right pictures can bring about the right changes in your life, the sooner you can attend interviews with confidence, the sooner you can perform well at examinations, and at work.

It all depends on what you picture, and how you picture it.

In creative imagery, use your imagination to create a clear image of some result or change you wish to bring about. Then continue to focus on the idea or picture regularly, until it becomes a reality. You will actually believe what you have been visualising, and this will be a good thing. If you believe yourself to be confident, see yourself in your mind as a confident person, you soon will be. See yourself attending important interviews, see yourself talking confidently at those occasions, and you will perform very well. See yourself giving public talks, believe that you are giving important talks to a hundred or so people in the audience, and you will be that person you believe you are. You have told your mind (through those positive mental pictures you have created) and it, in turn, will react accordingly. It won't let you down!

You want to be a good public speaker. Then think like a public speaker, speak like a public speaker, look like a public speaker, dress like a public speaker and visualise this from this moment that you are a good public speaker and you will be!

Whatever you visualise, experience it as if it is already happening.

But to achieve anything through visualisation, you must have an open mind that the desired changes are possible.

FOCUS ON THE DESIRABLE

Control the images that enter your mind—do not allow undesirable images into your mind. It is the pictures that you form that will change you for the better. Create undesirable pictures and hold them to the extent that your mind believes that that is what it is like (like failing that examination, reacting, performing poorly at that important job interview), then you will become just like you pictured yourself. Remember that a good picture is your greatest attribute in life. Anything you picture is yours, or can be yours. It is as simple as that.

But to medical researchers this phenomenon is not all that surprising. Much research time and a lot of research funding is spent on what is known in medical circles as the placebo effect. Placebos are, in effect, dud, ineffective medicines. They work as effectively as potent, expensive medication in about seventy or eighty percent of cases, and just as efficiently. Distilled water injected into the veins of the person believing it is a tranquilliser, will make that person feel dizziness and numb the senses as the 'tranquilliser' takes effect. And don't overlook the effectiveness of placebos. These same dud medications are as good as strong pain killers in relieving pain, and in promoting recovery.

The only difference, it seems, between the real thing and the dud medication, is that the recipient believes he or she is being given the real thing that is going to relieve them of their discomfort and distressing symptoms and severe pain. Because the mind has accepted what it believes, it works.

The recipients don't know what they have received. As long as they believe they have received something potent that they expect to work, then in most cases, it will work for them.

It is what they believe that works.

IT IS WHAT WE BELIEVE THAT COUNTS

And so too with creative imagery. If we create pictures that are strong enough, vivid enough, realistic enough, and appropriate enough, then the mind accepts the picture, the image, as if it has actually already happened.

In life, it is a strange irony that the simplest thing to fool is our own mind. We do it all the time. We really believe that we are going to goof that interview, fail that exam, make a mess of our new job. We fool ourselves all the time.

Visualising desired outcomes to achieve a positive result is no different to the process we used to create the situation we are in, our beliefs about ourselves that we have now. It is no different to dud pills killing the severe pain of broken bones. It is no different to what we already know about ourselves. Or do we? Or perhaps we only imagined that all those thoughts were true about us. Perhaps, really, they are not so.

I have considered so far two of the outstanding benefits of creative imagery — overcoming and reversing the conditioned responses we have developed and that restrict us in our everyday activities, and extending our expectations of what we are capable of doing.

During creative imagery, there are changes in the muscles that control our legs, our arms, our bodies. There are changes in the electrical stimulus of the neurons in our limbs. They act as if they are actually performing what it is the mind is visualising. They can't tell the difference between the two activities.

I have found that the more an activity is mentally rehearsed in total concentration, closing of the eyes and visualising the perfect result, how much better the activity is when performed. Practise whatever you want to do again and again. Do it for days. If it is important, visualise that activity for weeks if you can, and if the results warrant that much effort.

It is often much more pleasant visualising many situations than going through similar situations in real life — interviews, and anything else we must do. And the good thing about performing these situations in your mental images is that you do not suffer humiliation and setbacks, because you control the pictures — all of them — that you are creating, so the outcome can only be positive and successful.

Chapter 3 Visualisation

Visualisation is not a strange phenomenon out of some science fiction work. You picture something—catching a bus to work, arriving late and you picture the boss waiting at the door for you to explain your absence. In the past, many of us have used these images we create in a relatively unconscious way. From now on, the techniques outlined in this book will show you how to hold an image, and how to work with an image in a constructive, positive and successful way.

Now we can look at the technique of creating pictures of yourself in any situation and holding them. We are going to look at how to put yourself in that picture, and how you can see yourself performing what you want—enhancing your performance in sports, in study or at meetings, how to control those images, how to put yourself in the situation in which you now feel uncomfortable, and turn your feelings around so you feel at ease. You won't want to look back on the old you. That is one image that you will most likely want to forget.

Results of visualisation can take longer if we are battling with years of negativism and distrust in our lives. You must realise that you won't necessarily gain a great improvement in the first hours of using this technique. That's to be expected. Don't forget that you must, in many cases, overcome years, indeed often a lifetime, of behaviour, reaction, attitude that has created the situation that you will want to be changing in yourself. If you have been shy for thirty years, be reasonable and allow a little time for the effects to work. They will, that I will promise you — as long as you work at creating and holding the images of the results you desire to achieve or bring about in your life.

HOW LONG? NOT VERY LONG

Some conditions in which you now feel uncomfortable were created for you perhaps only recently. Take a grumpy boss who makes you feel intimidated merely by his presence, or by the sound of his voice. However, I have found repeatedly, that despite the time involved in creating the initial situation that led to your reaction — whether it was a week or half a lifetime — the time taken for the imaging to work and provide you with the desired benefits of this form of therapy, is only a matter of weeks.

Three weeks. Perhaps four. Yes, three or four weeks — perhaps a bit longer sometimes — is often all you will need to spend visualising each scene to evoke the desired results. There is a good reason for this time period. The mind does not incorporate that image immediately. This of course does not mean that after twenty-one days you stop visualising the desired results. Far from it. Keep visualising the desired outcome far beyond the time when you have experienced the desired change in your reaction to a situation, or have otherwise achieved the desired results. Keep those pictures forming until the desired result is really and truly part of you. Excessive imaging of an event or outcome is not harmful unless it becomes an obsession.

There is ample evidence that the mind really does take a little while to accept a change. Some people who have had a painful tooth extracted can feel the same pain after the extraction. In medical texts, there is a condition called the phantom limb syndrome. This refers to amputees who still feel their limb after the amputation. The pain is not there, but the mind believes it is, therefore the mind will feel the pain as if the troubled, broken or diseased limb is still there, causing the severe discomfort.

Visualisation

So don't rush the process, and don't give up. Wait out your time, practising, practising, practising.

This is not to say that you will always need the three-week time period to achieve any changes, nor is it always necessary to spend several weeks on bringing about every change you want to accomplish. Say you have to give a presentation to your colleagues at work next week. You are nervous when asked. You only have five days, and you tell yourself that this is not sufficient time, because you read that you need at least three weeks.

You will need three weeks or more to bring about long-lasting and significant changes for the better. You will, or should, experience significant changes with only a few sessions of visualisation. So if you have five days, make the most of them. I often have only one day's warning about a forthcoming (previously) threatening situation. I find this is quite sufficient to bring about the desired state of mind so that at the time, I am confident, relaxed, and as if I am only repeating what I have done many times before.

Even if I have only a short time before I interview someone, this is sufficient for me to picture the room, the table, all the furniture in place, what the person might look like. I can relate to them easily because I have done it so many times before I meet them.

Before you start visualising what you want to bring about, be clear about what it is you want to achieve. If you visualise conflicting scenes, the results could be rather interesting. Make sure that each image only enhances those you have created before it. Don't, for example, visualise yourself getting on well with your boss, only seconds later picturing yourself feeling threatened by him or seeing yourself doing him malicious harm! The pictures must all be consistent with the desired result.

CREATE A NEW PHOTOGRAPHIC ALBUM

Under no circumstances should you allow undesirable images into your mind, those images that, if they were photographs of yourself, you would be embarrassed to show even to your best friends! See all the images that you create from now on as photographs, and have on display in your album in your mind only those that you are proud of. What pictures would you show? It's easy to throw out a lot of images that we would rather not know about from now on. It is unfortunate that many people carry around with them a bulging album of all those photographs, often taken way back in the early parts of their lives, and keep them on permanent display where they can see them all the time. Throw them out and put in their place a whole set of new pictures.

One of the enjoyable things about visualisation (apart from the tremendous benefits you will experience within a very short time) is that you can practise visualisation almost anywhere. Although a relaxed physical and mental state is preferable, it is by no means the only way you will be able to achieve desired outcomes through visualisation. I find moments of boredom very productive. There will always be tasks that need to be done, whether at home, during work, or while playing sport, when your mind tends to wander onto more enjoyable themes. These are the times when you can gain tremendous benefit from visualisation. Even travelling by train or bus—thirty minutes when you are forced to sit there without being able to do much other than read a book. Moments like these are great to bring about the results you want. Visualisation does not have to be practised at the same time every day, as if it were a habit. Don't waste those precious moments we all have throughout our days. Make visualisation part of your life, each moment that you can spare, to bring about the desired changes.

Set aside whatever time you can afford each and every day for your visualisation. Aim for at least two periods a day, more if possible, in a quiet place where you won't be disturbed. Point

Visualisation

out to your family that you don't want to be disturbed during this time. If your family doesn't appreciate what you are aiming for, try to find a quiet spot away from all other people for the duration of these exercises. If you look hard enough, such a place won't be difficult to find. If your family does appreciate the reasons for your request for peace and quiet, then you can consider yourself fortunate. But if you cannot find lengthy periods for yourself, don't despair, because the techniques are just about as effective with several short bursts during the day or evening. Some people consider that several short periods are more beneficial to them than one or two long periods, because they find their mind is always tending to be active in imaging, and the pictures are with them for much of the day, even when they are not trying hard to form the pictures in their mind.

Bring your ideas or your images to mind often, both in quiet periods, and also casually throughout the day. In this way, you live the image, you breathe it, and you become it. That old saying that practice makes perfect was never truer than when applied to visualisation. There is no rule that says it has to be practised for a minimum of half an hour three times a day. Two minutes here, three minutes over a cup of morning tea, half an hour sitting in the park at lunchtime, ten minutes on the bus in the morning—all these small amounts of time are valuable, and most enjoyable.

So when we create images, what are we really trying to do?

It's a matter of creating an image of the desired outcome. If, for example, you feel threatened by your boss's loud voice, or by his large figure, the desired outcome, of course, is to be in a position where you are not threatened by his presence, and you accept his presence in a calm, self-assured way. One way might be to change jobs, but that is not always easy or practical. Anyway, it is possible you might end up with a boss in your new place of employment whose loud voice threatens you, or whose large figure intimidates you. It is much easier, more

In Your New Image

practical, and saves a lot more effort, if you change your reaction on hearing his loud voice, or seeing his large figure.

Picture the outcome as already existing, and the way you want it to be, with yourself in it, looking out—as if you are seeing the new scene through your own eyes. This is the result you want, so this is the one you will concentrate on—you feel at ease with your boss who has a loud voice and a large figure.

Sounds easy? It is!

Perhaps it is because it is so easy—some would say too easy—that many people will not even try it. Others dismiss it by saying something so easy could not work. Unfortunately those are the people who won't try it, will talk others out of trying it for themselves, and dismiss the whole process as a waste of time. It is a pity that those are the people who see things through only their eyes. Perhaps that is why many people like that are where they are in life, other than where they could be if they had an open mind.

One of the main reasons why visualisation fails is because people create a desirable image once or twice, or over perhaps two or three days, feel no immediate benefit, and give up.

Others create vivid pictures once of what they want, then negate the benefits by switching to something else, often a series of images that conflict with the outcome they really want to achieve. It is easy to see why the mind is confused, and for those people, visualisation does not work.

WHERE CAN YOU RELAX? ANYWHERE YOU LIKE

Start by creating images that are easy to form and hold. Begin by relaxing. Unlike hypnosis where a great degree of relaxation is required, with visualisation, relaxation to the same state is not required. Indeed, just being comfortable sitting at a desk, sitting under a tree or on a bus is quite a sufficient degree of relaxation to enable you to form detailed images.

Visualisation

At first you may find difficulty developing clear images, but they will come if you let them. If at first you picture little, do not give up, but take your time, even if you let your mind wander for a moment or two.

Close your eyes, and relax. Let your arms and legs relax by letting all the tension go from your muscles. Naturally, if you are sitting at a desk at work, you can't let go of every muscle, otherwise your boss would be justified in using his loud voice on you. If you are sitting down, relax enough to be comfortable. Your muscles should not be tense.

For some of the scenarios described in this book, almost complete relaxation is desired. These are the ones where, through conditioning from way back in your life, you tend to tense up, to cringe, to mentally withdraw.

For others, such as expanding your endurance in cycling, running, learning to weld or making a cabinet, relaxation to the same degree is not quite so essential.

The reason for at least a certain degree of relaxation is because muscular tension is providing input to your brain. Anything you feel against your back, a stick poking into your leg, a tight-fitting shoe, is a stimulus that will provide an impulse that will find its way to the brain as a signal and could form a distraction. Simply relax enough to lower the amount of input your brain has to cope with.

By reducing the physical tension, we automatically reduce the mental tension, and input or signals going to the brain, or what we have come to describe as anxiety. It is easy to see how, in such situations, both physical and mental tension work together to escalate the overall condition that you experience.

CREATE YOUR PICTURES

Your first image is going to be easy. Picture a nice, long, white sandy beach, with the water gently lapping the sand. Now hold that picture for as long as you can.

In Your New Image

There is no harm done if at first the picture lasts only a few seconds and then fades. Try to reform that picture again—the white beach and the water. Now hold it.

You might not be a beach person. Then picture something that to you is pleasurable. It might be a field you saw once in the country, or the autumn leaves in a park. Create whatever scene is pleasurable to you. But for this exercise, we will assume that you do like the beach and have formed a clear picture in your mind of the white sand and the water lapping gently against the edge.

Keep trying with this simple picture. It might take minutes for you to get the idea, it might take you weeks if you are not familiar with or used to working with mental pictures.

Let's move on and assume you have been able to create that simple scene and hold it for several minutes.

Now do something in that picture. Look at that scene as if you are walking along the sand—you will see the scene change. Imagine a seagull having landed some distance off. Make that scene as vivid and as real as it is possible to get it. Imagine the sound of the water lapping the sand. Can you hear it? What does it sound like? Keep walking. There is a small headland towards the end of the beach. Walk towards it. It might take you ten minutes to get there in your mind. Keep picturing that beach as you first saw it—hear the sounds if you can, see the ever-changing pattern of light, the clouds above you.

When you can visualise something like this scene (or another one that you chose instead of the beach scene), then you have the idea of what is involved.

When, in your picture, you are nearing the headland, try turning around and walking back to where you started. See the beach stretching out some way in front of you. See the sand in front of you. See the water now on the other side of you, and picture the clouds again.

Keep this scene simple until this type of picture comes to you easily and naturally. If at first it is difficult, or lasts only a few

Visualisation

seconds, then keep trying until you can hold a scene such as this for about five minutes or more.

Do not move on to create other images about the aspects of yourself that you want to change until you have got this right. You will be disappointed if the best you can do with holding the image is only a few seconds.

So practise this simple scene often—almost to the point where your reaction is that you have seen the beach so often that it's about time you visited it next weekend. That, then, is the time to move on to the next part of this exercise.

Create that image of the beach again. Now put yourself in that picture. Before, you were seeing the beach through your own eyes—you possibly could not see yourself on the beach as you were walking along. But now you will see yourself through another person's eyes walking along the sand towards that distant headland.

Imaging yourself—perhaps in clothes that you would reasonably wear on a beach in weather such as that in the picture you are creating—light top and shorts if it is warm and sunny. You are seeing this person who is yourself. Watch yourself walk. You see the person bend over to pick up a shell, hold it for a few seconds and then throw it away.

Did you see this person looking at the shell? Then practise the scene over again until you do. This is important, because unless you can see yourself in the pictures, and move that person, make yourself bend over, pat a dog, look up at the clouds, put your hand in the water—then you will not get the full benefit from visualisation.

You must—and I emphasise this—you must be able to create pictures that you can manipulate. They must not be static. You must learn how to bring in elements and take out elements. You must control the movement in the scenes every time. You must be in full control of all the action in every image every time.

Don't treat this part of the exercise lightly, for without it, the other benefits you would otherwise achieve with visualisation will be slow in forthcoming.

Creating the proper image is important, and so is patience.

Patience will allow you to develop the right technique throughout all the scenarios I have described later in the book. You may have skimmed through the pages, seen some scenarios that appeal to you and in which you can identify yourself. How long have you felt shy? How long have you felt embarrassed with members of the opposite sex? Years? Decades? Then one or two more weeks are not going to hurt you now, despite your eagerness to start changing things in your life for the better.

The greatest benefit from the images you form will come to you if those pictures are as realistic as it is possible for the best artist in the world to make them. They have to be true to life — the sounds, the colours, the feel of the air, the feel of the environment, the setting. The image has to win a prestigious painting prize that is awarded for its accuracy and realistic effects. Don't overlook any detail. With some of the scenarios, it might be desirable to spend a few minutes extra at the beginning of each session just to ensure that you have added all the furniture in the office, the picture on your lounge room wall, the cushions on the sofa where you will be with your new-found friend you have taken home for coffee. Picture every detail. Don't overlook a thing.

Say you are learning a new skill, like welding. You have had one or two lessons in welding to get the feel of using the equipment, know what the welding equipment sounds like, the hum, the sound of the splatter of the metal being deposited. Get the right feel.

If you get just the taste of welding, you can visualise the glow, the smoke, hear the crackle in your mind. This is what you want. In your mind, go over and over the task. Say you are welding. Create a few mistakes, put mistakes into the work, go back and correct them. You know how it should be done.

Visualisation

For carpentry — hold the image of yourself cutting some wood, or nailing or drilling the timber. See the piece of furniture you are making, hear the sound of the electric drill, take special notice of the screws on the work bench, and the nails by your elbow.

Why does your picture — whatever you are visualising — have to be so detailed, so realistic? Your mind has to believe that the circumstances you are visualising are real. Your mind won't accept them unless it believes they are real.

With all the scenes we will be creating throughout this book, it is important to visualise the desired outcome, not the situation as it exists at present. If you concentrate on the present situation — feeling intimidated by the boss with the large figure, then your outcome will be to feel intimidated by the same boss. The desired outcome in this scenario is not to feel intimidated by that same boss, but to feel relaxed and comfortable in his presence. This is the outcome you will be striving for, therefore you will concentrate on feeling happy with him nearby. So the images you create will be those of sitting with him, talking with him, perhaps having a cup of coffee on the opposite side of his desk while the two of you chat together in congenial conversation.

Before beginning any visualisation as you work through any of the scenarios that interest you, it is essential you identify very clearly exactly what your desired outcome really is. This will not only help you focus on what the problem is, but will help narrow the range of images you need to create and work with in your mind to achieve the results for which you are reading this book.

I would suggest that you list on paper firstly what the problem is, secondly, the setting, or settings, and thirdly, what you would like the result to be if you had the power to change the world any way you were able. Don't forget, with visualisation, many things are possible.

In Your New Image

Be sensible. If you really detest you boss (remember, you are not alone in the world in this regard!) it is not practical nor sensible to say you would like to shoot him so you can get a new boss. This would not achieve much, and the new boss might be worse. That too is possible. That is what I referred to in chapter one when I talked about freedom. You can be free of people like these in your life, because through visualisation, you can develop the skills and the confidence and the courage to change your situation and yourself so that you can confidently leave situations like these that do nothing for your self esteem or self respect.

FOCUS ON WHAT YOU WANT

Just as visualisation is of tremendous benefit to moving forward and achieving a great deal in your life, undesirable visualisation—that is, visualising, constantly, pictures that are undesirable—is harmful. Think about it for a moment. If you can achieve positive changes in your life through positive images, the opposite is also true. If you dwell on undesirable outcomes, then undesirable outcomes will surely result. That is how powerful visualisation can be! Concentrate instead only on circumstances you are trying to achieve. Eliminate all other undesirable scenes that are irrelevant, as they come to your mind. It is likely that other images will come to you while you are relaxing. Unless they contribute, or are likely to contribute, to the outcomes that you are desiring, put them aside and concentrate only on those you want. You may wish to develop the other images later if you think they will lead to changes that will be beneficial to you.

So the setting here that you would identify with would be something like this.

I feel intimidated every time I see or hear my boss. I inwardly tremble whenever I see his form coming out of his office

Visualisation

towards my desk. I seize up as he walks towards me, even if I know he is not coming to criticise me.

The result you want is quite different to the setting that you already are familiar with.

The setting you describe on paper could be described something like this.

I want to feel relaxed and confident whenever I see my boss. I do not want to feel threatened any more. I have had enough of my reaction to him. And remember, yours is only a reaction to him. Other staff members might feel quite at ease with the same person. Perhaps you were conditioned to feel uncomfortable with men of large build.

Now you can start visualising the right outcome, creating an image of what you want to happen.

This is how you can achieve it.

Concentrate on one scenario at a time, especially in the early stages of learning this technique. It will help focus on your desired goal without the confusion or distraction of trying to take on too many different types of images or situations all at once. I am not saying though that, with considerable practice and experience, you will not be able to combine two or even three quite different scenarios and achieve a high degree of success. But, let's begin to walk before we do anything else.

Start by creating images that are easy to form and hold.

Picture the outcome as already existing, and the way you want it to be, with yourself in it, looking out — as if you are seeing the new scene through your own eyes. It will be realistic — you are looking at the world through your own eyes, just as you would be in real life. This is what you want to happen.

But let's practise with our scenario involving our threatening boss. First, relax yourself by picturing a pleasant scene — such as the sandy beach and the water gently lapping the edge of the sand.

Hold this image for perhaps a couple of minutes, even picture walking along the beach towards that distant headland.

Remember, at all times during this visualising exercise, you should remain physically calm and relaxed.

Now imagine your boss on the beach a long way ahead of you. You see him, you recognise him, but he is too far off to be of any threat to you. You continue, in your visualisation, to walk in his direction, still feeling quite calm.

You get closer to him. What is he wearing? Is he in shorts? An open-neck shirt? Wearing sandals? Is his hair blown about in the warm, gentle breeze that is blowing on the beach? Picture him in as much detail as you can. What is he doing? Is he looking out towards the horizon? Is he bending down to pick up a shell? Do not react to his presence — merely see him there, in the distance.

You are still physically relaxed and calm. That is what you want to achieve.

The two of you walk slowly towards one another. You must still remain physically calm and relaxed — again, I must stress that you must not react to his presence.

You approach. You are still relaxed. He smiles at you. You return his greeting, remaining physically calm while this is occurring.

He says hello. You return his greeting and keep walking.

You continue to walk on along the beach towards the distant headland.

You return along the way you have come after reaching that headland.

There he is in the distance, walking slowly towards you once more. Again, you are physically relaxed, and you do not react at all on seeing him there. You observe his presence, and that is all.

Watch him slowly get closer to you. He is not a threat to you at all, so you remain calm. The two of you meet again. He stops, smiles, and talks to you again. You exchange conversation for a short time, and go on your respective ways.

Visualisation

Now return to the beach scene without your boss there in view. You are still relaxed, enjoying the scene in front of you. You amble along the sand, looking at the water, feeling the warmth of the sunshine on your back. End this scene.

Don't get up quickly after an experience of relaxation such as the one you have just achieved. Remain there for perhaps a minute or two, take a few deep breaths to regain your full stamina, move you hands and arms, then stretch your legs, maybe your back and neck before rousing completely out of your state of physical (and hopefully mental) relaxation.

If you can achieve this simple visualisation quickly and easily, it is time to move on and put more depth into your visualisation exercises. If you were nervous when you imagined your boss there on the beach with you, practise the exercise again and again up to this point until you feel quite comfortable at seeing him there. There is no point in moving on to the next part until you can get this first part right.

But take your time. You didn't become conditioned to men with large frames only yesterday, so what is a delay of another couple of days going to make to you?

But let's assume you have practised and practised this part of the exercise so that you can see your boss there on the beach with you without his presence instilling any fear in you.

SAME PEOPLE, DIFFERENT PEOPLE

After you see him on the beach in your mind, try switching the scene to your office. Picture yourself sitting at your desk. What is around you? What colours are the walls? Is there a picture on your wall? A calendar? Is there a clock, or are there papers or posters or notices pinned to the wall next to your desk? Make this scene as vivid and as real as possible.

You are quite relaxed physically. Your boss's office is empty. You look around. He is not in your office either. Remaining quite calm and relaxed, put him in the picture. Put him sitting at his desk, or somewhere else where you can see him in the distance. You watch him for a few minutes but without experiencing any sort of reaction to him. He is there, and that is all there is to the picture. If you feel you are starting to tighten up, try relaxing again.

Watch him, again with indifference.

He stands up, but you remain physically relaxed and calm. Watch him as he moves towards your desk. He is bringing some papers over for you to look at. Whatever you do, do not tighten up. You should remain calm.

He stands next to your desk. Again, you are quite indifferent to his presence next to you. You show no emotion at all — he is there, and you are sitting at your desk.

Now let him talk to you. See his lips moving. Hear what he has to say. Listen to him. Let the movements be slow, so that you can adjust yourself to the changing scene unfolding in front of you.

He reaches out and passes you some papers. You reach out, smile, and accept them. You should still be calm and relaxed. You should be quite indifferent to his presence, not intimidated, not fearing anything from him.

Watch him return to his office and sit down. Watch him, without feeling anything. Just ... see him there in the office in front of you, minding his own business. See this scene for perhaps a minute or two.

Now you can return to the beach scene and continue your walk along the white sand towards the headland. Let yourself be roused out of this state of relaxation first by taking a few deep breaths, then a gentle stretch before getting up.

If time permits of course, there is no harm done by continuing to sit or lie there, relaxed, and imagining this scene over again. You will only get more benefit if you practise it several times.

Let us go back over the main lesson of this chapter. The main points are:

Visualisation

- clearly identify the situation that you want to improve (as it exists now)
- determine the desired outcome as vividly as you can (how you would like the situation to be)
- ascertain what pictures you will need to create to achieve the desired outcome.

THAT'S NOT ALL YOU CAN DO

Let us now turn to two other types of situations that you may wish to work on.

Say you want to write a book. You know you have the skills to at least draft the manuscript. You have considerable experience in the subject (or the book might be a novel or a collection of short stories that you are good at writing, or how-to articles that you want to share with readers). You would see yourself sitting at the computer, excited, typing quickly to get the thoughts down as they come to you. You would picture the desired result — seeing the manuscript finished, with you putting it in the envelope and sending it to your publisher. You would picture yourself seeing the book in the book stores or opening the magazine or journal and seeing your article featured. Concentrate on the desired outcomes at all times, as well as the processes that are certain to take you and your achievements to that point of success. If you concentrate on images of this type long enough, you will be surprised at the success you should be able to attain.

If you practise these techniques to achieve the desired outcomes, bear in mind that too much of a good thing is not always good for you overall. If you lose your fear of camping, don't for goodness sake completely lose your fear of wild animals. If you are camping where wild animals are known to be roaming, don't be so relaxed as to say on hearing a roar that

In Your New Image

it is only a bear and do nothing about it. You must be sensible, and find the compromise.

But let us concentrate on the achievable. Let us now look at how we can make those changes so we see ourselves as capable, secure, confident individuals who fit in with our environment, our society, our new expectations of ourselves and make something rewarding and satisfying of our lives.

Chapter 4 Your Self Image

Since there is considerable evidence based on innumerable claims that a good self image is the most important asset that we possess, what is the best way to ensure that we each have a good picture of ourselves? We can start with the basics, and work up from there. This exercise, if you are not one of those lucky people who already possesses such a self image, will be the most important in this book. The other scenarios will only enhance the improvements you will soon experience through carrying out the exercises here.

A poor self image can reveal itself in any number of undesirable ways. The common manifestations include anger, anti-social behaviour, violence, domestic violence against your loved ones, or just complaining that the world is a terrible place to live in, and anyway, it owes me a living!

Probably the greatest single determinant of what you will be or do with your creative abilities is your perception of who you are — the weaker your self image, the less you will be capable of achieving. Self esteem is central to the whole problem of securing any type of success in any endeavour. No one is capable of reaching beyond the limits of his or her own self-imposed boundaries. Unfortunately, most of us have been taught to sell ourselves short. We certainly don't start out in life that way.

It does not matter if there is any real substance to the image we have of ourselves. What is important is that we believe it to be so.

It is as simple as that. It is how we see ourselves that matters more than anything else in this world, what we are, and how we are, and often where we are in life.

A person with a very poor self image but who is very intelligent might make nothing of their life, whereas someone who is of moderate intelligence and possesses a great self image will get on with their life and soar ahead and pass all of the others on the road to success. Even mountains won't slow these people down. But the ones with a poor self image? They are still nursing themselves along because they never even made it as far as the mountain. Have pride in yourself and your successes. If not, imagine yourself with pride.

Visualisation will overcome that poor self image and help you overcome just about all the major barriers between where you are now and where you would like to be.

An attractive appearance, a fine body and being the 'correct height' don't really mean that much. The most beautiful woman is not necessarily the most confident, the most assured person, the happiest woman. Often they are, but those who are not considered to be the most attractive can be the most poised women, have tremendous confidence, and ability attributable to their self confidence (and self image). So don't turn away from the rewards that can await you simply because you are not the most handsome fellow in town, or the most glamorous woman in your part of the world.

YOUR SELF IMAGE—YOUR SUCCESS

Your self image is your key to your success. You will perform exactly as you see yourself. Some people are defeatists. A poor self image is their worst enemy. How we really fit in with reality is our understanding of who we are, and the fear of losing touch with reality is a very traumatic one. As we saw earlier, all of us

Your Self Image

have a tendency to cling to beliefs about ourselves, and those strengths and weaknesses we possess. The result is a self-fulfilling prophecy, where our beliefs about what we can do determine what we actually do. We are often governed by those around us, sometimes saying what if, it can't be done, you might get hurt, you might fall, you might not succeed, you might lose your way, don't do it. Unfortunately those with good intentions often fail to add 'I wouldn't do that because I am scared, but you should go ahead. Please don't be like me, don't end up like I have.' With an improved self image, all that changes for the better.

Most of us have been conditioned to think of ourselves as unimaginative and uncreative. We only need to dwell on our childhood for a few minutes to realise where those ideas came from! Until that hurdle is cleared, little can come of your own creative efforts. You simply have to believe in your creative abilities, and believe in yourself, before you can begin to reap meaningful benefits from the real you.

BE YOURSELF—NOT SOMEONE ELSE

Don't let other people define your creativity, or your other potential. No one, including you, knows what you are capable of doing or thinking up until you have tried, tried and tried some more. Many believed that Mount Everest was impossible to climb. Then, on one day alone only recently, there were thirty-seven climbers on the summit of the mountain. All because they didn't accept that the mountain was impossible to climb. We are not capable of achieving that which we believe is impossible. Do you believe that any one of those climbers on the summit on that one day believed they would never have climbed to the top? I doubt if even one of them would have had negative thoughts about their success that day.

It is a sad fate of many of us that we are governed by what we think other people want us to do. Parents set goals for us — their goals. They tell us to go into teaching, or work in a bank, when we don't want to. We take their 'advice', accept that it was offered in our best interests, and accept that as our future, resign ourselves to the fact that there is nothing else out there, no purpose, nothing refreshing and original to do, see, be. Our self esteem and worth diminishes over time. It is time to decide your future and go for it. Together we will make changes — I will give you all the principles I have learned and developed over a lifetime of living, and give you what I have learned from my research and from years of helping other people become achievers through visualisation. Your job is easy, and that is to get on with what you want to do, be. Decide where you are going, and realise what it will take you to get you there. The easy way through life is to follow the crowd, to forget your ideas and be like all the others. Don't climb that mountain. Stay at home. Be one of the crowd.

Few of us have the vision to realise what is possible. Without a sound self image, few of us will ever achieve for ourselves anything more than the merest that is expected from us in our routine lives.

The assumptions (that is, your 'beliefs', whether true or false) you make about yourself will determine to what extent you develop fully in this life of yours. As I said, no one knows what you are capable of — yet.

IS THAT ALL I CAN EXPECT IN LIFE? NO!

Few of us have the vision to realise what is possible. The impossible is what we accept — our limitations that we impose, it's that holding back from life when we really could surge forward, it is saying no to life when there is so much to do and achieve through our own efforts. We tell ourselves what is impossible. It's when we lack the courage to try something new, lack the courage to change jobs to get one that is more meaningful, its lacking the courage to branch out on our own

Your Self Image

when things at work are pretty flat. Courage can move mountains. Not many people have the courage necessary, consequently not many mountains get moved. Courage could change each of us for the better. Truly no one knows what you are capable of. But through visualisation ... who knows?

Your future is where you are going to spend the rest of your life. How do you feel about that prospect? Would you be happy to live in your present circumstances for the next twenty, or perhaps fifty years? Would you be disappointed if someone were to say to you, I am going to wave a magic wand and I am going to change your circumstances, the way you feel about yourself. Would you like that? It amazes me how many people are indifferent to their present lifestyle, uncaring that they are now entering their future phase of life. Yet what you do now can determine the rest of your life. Look at the people in the street walking past you on any week day. Do they look happy? Are many of them full of life? Enthusiastic? Full of energy? Do they look alive? And on a weekend, are the expressions on their faces any different?

Most likely they look forlorn, sorrowful, dismayed at their present circumstances, yet oblivious to the means to change their lot as they enter their future. It would, in twenty years time, I am sure, dismay them even further if they could look back and accept that they had the chance all those years earlier to have changed their circumstances, changed their self image, and put more joy and living into their lives. They did have the chance to change things. That time was called now.

I have discussed the almost magic powers that visualisation can bring to your life. If you want it to. It can make changes to the way you see yourself. If you want it to. It can give you courage and confidence so that setbacks in life don't really bother you. If you want it that way. It can change just about everything you do now but are not happy with, your approach to your daily living, your approach to your work colleagues, to your work, your recreation, your family. If you want it to do so.

But a lot of people we all meet are reluctant to change, even for the better. They feel secure in the sameness, the routine of their lives, the drabness of their surroundings. They don't want change because, as we saw earlier, to them sameness is security.

But by changing your self image, building your confidence, changing your attitude through changing your self image, all the rest of these things around you and about you that might not be perfect today can change too.

START SMALL, END BIG

As I said, start with the basics. List on a piece of paper all — and I mean all — the good things you have done in your whole life. Okay, I know that if you feel badly about yourself, you are going to say that won't take very long, but you are wrong. Put a lot of thought into it, and write down all you can think of for the list. Like what? Like the day you did very well in an examination you weren't expecting to pass by much way back when you were at school. Like the time you managed to take your family on a low, low budget holiday and ensured that they all had a great time. You might remember the praises from your family about giving them so much with so little expense. Like the dinner you cooked when your husband brought his boss around for dinner unannounced, and the boss gave you genuine praise for your superb efforts. Like the time you won the race at the athletics carnival at school, or raised more money than the other committee members of the board you are on. Like the time you crafted something and got endless praises from your colleagues at work for making something fantastic.

I think you will get the picture now.

You might have put such incidents out of your mind — they might have happened too far back, perhaps at a time in your life when circumstances, the people you associated with, were different. So you might have to struggle for a while to come up with anything that is more than a chicken scratching. But go

Your Self Image

back, day by day — do a fast scroll back through your life — to recall all those events. Don't dismiss them just because, nowadays, they might seem small and even insignificant. It is obvious that since you can remember them, they were important to you at the time, and they certainly are important to you right now. They will be even more important to you by the time you have read to the end of this chapter. It may be that, right now, those events that were important to you at the time were overshadowed by more recent or current events in your life. The aim here is to think beyond the present and recall all the good things you have done, or that have happened to you.

Aim for a list with at least twenty items on it. If you think of more, that's good. But don't worry if it takes you a month to compile the list, just do it. Anyway, if it takes you a month to compile the list, the hard part is almost over. Keep the list open. Add to it whenever you recall another of those good moments in your life.

Make sure that all the events on your list are times that you really felt good. This is important. Consider each of them very carefully.

Now go about memorising them, or record the list onto a tape with long pauses between each item for recalling each moment in its grandeur, and play it back — the duration of the tape should be as long as you have available for this exercise. A sixty to ninety minute tape recorded on only one side would be fine if you can find that amount of time when you know you won't be disturbed.

People who succeed have a good self image. Those who fail usually have a poor self image. Look around you. Are those successful people amongst your work colleagues shrivelled up inside themselves? I doubt it! Are your friends who are outgoing, shrivelled up in how they see themselves? I doubt that too! Are the failures, the non-achievers, those who aim very low, who expect little, endowed with a good self image? And I doubt that also, for the two categories are almost mutually

In Your New Image

exclusive. In other words, we cannot be a success if we see ourselves badly, and we cannot be failures if we see ourselves in a positive light and with a glowing self image.

I am not including here mere setbacks — we all suffer those from time to time. The difference, though, is that those with a good self image will get up again using their inner strengths and rise above their temporary defeat. Or, on the other hand, if our self image is so poor, the setback reinforces what we thought of ourselves. I told you so, and here's proof, it is saying to those people. After you have applied the principles laid down in this book, you too should be able to rise above setbacks and soar above the inconvenience and shoot far ahead. That's the difference your new self image is going to make to you, your future, your ambitions and your successes.

Instead of trying to manipulate the outside world to make it what would be perfect in your opinion, it is far easier, quicker, and the results better, if you can change yourself and the image you have of yourself.

IS THE PROBLEM WITH YOU, OR WITH THE REST OF THE WORLD?

My wife and I recently went to a restaurant for lunch in a small country town near our home. It was a cold day in mid-winter, and there were not many people eating there. Near us at the next table was a young couple, talking to each other, holding hands. Next to them was an older couple, also holding hands for much of the time they were at the restaurant. My wife remarked that it was a pleasant change to see happy people, actually enjoying themselves. They were pleasant, talking to each other softly, laughing, obviously enjoying each other's company immensely.

Opposite us was another couple. Both looked unhappy, barely talking during their meal, he sitting with his arms folded when he wasn't eating, frowning, defiant. The woman

Your Self Image

complained about the meal, although the food at the restaurant was of a very high standard and served with efficiency and a genuine smile. Nothing was too much for the waiters that afternoon. The man, just before he left the table, called the waiter over and complained about all the things he had found wrong with his meal. These were two people whom I can assume were unhappy with themselves, therefore there was something wrong, in both their minds, with the world. On that day, the meal wasn't good enough for them. Tomorrow, well, anything could have gone wrong for this couple.

But if you were to ask them, both these people would have denied that the problem lay entirely with themselves. We all know there are problems of numerous sorts in the world — lack of jobs, the high cost of living, political systems everywhere in chaos, financial systems failing, and so on. But if we are happy within ourselves, then these outside influences don't seem to matter so much. I am not saying they can be forgotten, just played down to their right perspective in our individual lives. But on that day at that charming restaurant, the couple were not happy. It was the world that was wrong. They blamed something beyond themselves instead of looking within themselves for the answer. That is where we will often find something wrong, and the seat of most of our problems in life. From within.

I cannot understand why people harbour so many negative images of themselves. After all, positive images are just as easy to form in the mind as are negative ones. The results are vastly different. I believe the difference is that most people have not been shown the benefits of positive images of themselves. Perhaps that is the only difference between successful people and those who are considered unsuccessful.

In Your New Image

YOUR SELF IMAGE MAKES YOU WHAT YOU ARE

The self image is the foundation of our whole personality. Because of this, our experiences seem to verify, and thereby strengthen our self images. What we do relates to the way we see ourselves. It is almost as if we have a constant picture of what we are and react accordingly. And that is exactly the way it is with our minds. But think for a moment what we would be like if that picture were to change. Instead of the present picture we have of ourselves, imagine what we would be like if we saw ourselves differently.

Have you ever noticed the difference in behaviour in a person who changes some aspect of their outside appearance? Sometimes merely growing a moustache can make a vast difference to a man's personality, a new hairstyle can lift a person's self esteem.

I once worked with a person, a young man who was shy and who had a stutter that wasn't very noticeable except perhaps to himself and his immediate friends. He was well liked, mainly, I feel, because of his pleasant personality, but he fitted in well with whatever his circumstances were.

Several years later I moved to another city. I knew he had moved too, but I had lost touch with him. I joined an outdoors club, and started hearing rumours about a person with the same name as my friend. I knew it wasn't him because his personality did not fit the rumours I was hearing. They were rather distressing. One of the complaints was that his arrogance was outright dangerous in the outdoors, his 'couldn't care less about others' attitude had left several people stranded in dangerous icy conditions. Some time later I ran into the person with the same name as my previous friend.

Unfortunately it was the same person, but the new one had grown a beard, saw himself differently, perhaps was hiding his true self behind the beard, and had become a totally different person. Interestingly, he had lost his shyness and his stammer. But he did not have to grow a beard to change his self image.

Your Self Image

And unfortunately it was a sad case of his seeing himself as the wrong type of person.

YOUR SELF IMAGE MUST BE A TRUE IMAGE

A lot of our ideas about ourselves will be self fulfilling unless we change our self image. We know we will fail that important examination, so we come close to the pass mark. We know we won't get that job, and we don't. We know we won't be happy in any activity we take part in, and, once again, our predictions are correct. Naturally they are. We forecast the outcome well in advance. There is not another outcome likely to result from the incorrect images we carry around of ourselves, day after day, year after year. Naturally it is easy to see the future. It's as bleak as we want to make it. But why not change? It's easy.

A lot of our ideas are so well ingrained in our minds that we will argue that the person telling us otherwise is wrong. We really believe in ourselves, in what we see. Unfortunately we see what others have told us, have ingrained in our subconscious mind, we believe it because at the time their remarks fitted our actions, therefore the person, or people, must have been right. But they weren't. We are the ones who have to carry their incorrect assessment of us. Often their assessment of us is based on very flimsy evidence, one small incident perhaps, one clumsy moment when we spilled the soup in the visitor's lap. Often their summing up of us is incorrectly based on their incorrect idea and assessment of themselves. They see others being like them. Now, that is no recommendation, is it—to be like the average person? Couldn't you do better than that for yourself? Do you want to be just average, because others have decided you fit the mould of their ill-conceived perception of people? Were they an impeccable judge of character? Probably not. So why take their opinions of yourself and accept them as your own?

No, if this sounds like you, then it is definitely time to get a new picture of yourself, and a new life for yourself.

CHANGE YOUR SELF IMAGE AND THE WORLD SINGS ALONG WITH YOU

Once the idea of self is changed, other things consistent with this new concept may be accomplished often without great strain. Every action, every thought, complies with the new image. Nothing could be easier. It's almost as easy—and as pleasant—as having several dreams every night for the next few weeks of your successes, you, confident, you, without that stammer and weak voice when you talk.

Your good self image will be with you through thick and thin, through bad times to get you through, and remain with you through all the good times you will experience.

If you believe that you could never become the person you want to become, it's time to change your self image. Well, let me reassure you that that old self image belonged to yesterday.

Once the idea of self is changed, other things consistent with this new concept may be accomplished—often without great strain or pain. Everything in life will tend to fall into place, in a way that is consistent with that new image of yourself.

Your new self image can be the best asset that you will ever possess. With a good self image, you can go places, do things you never dreamed possible. But with that old, worn out self image that is not fit for today's living? Well, forget that one. It's not going to do you any good. The poor self image hasn't done you very much good up to now, so why not change it? Well, let me reassure you that that was yesterday. From today as you work through this book, things are about to change for you, so you had better hang on tight!

Self-acceptance, through a good, strong self image, is the foundation of a peaceful mind. And with that, you will be able to clear the greatest hurdle of life with a single bound.

Your Self Image

This is how you can improve your self image through visualisation.

LEARN TO PICTURE ALL YOUR PAST SUCCESSES IN LIFE

Picture a beach scene, with you walking along the white sand, with the water gently lapping the shore. Hold this scene for at least a couple of minutes until you can really feel yourself there, and feel the warmth of the imaginary sun on your back.

Now picture that first event on your list. Picture it as vividly as if it were happening again right now. Picture it in all its original detail that you can recall. Do you remember how good you felt about it? Do you recall just how people beamed at you at that success? Hold that image and the feel of that occasion for a few minutes.

Return to the beach scene briefly.

Now picture the second item of past successes on your list. Do you recall how you felt when you had accomplished that? Do you remember the joy you experienced after that event? Recall how you felt. Hold that image for a few minutes, and more importantly, hold that feeling you experienced at that time. This too is very important.

Return to the beach scene between visualising each of the events on your list. This will help you to maintain that relaxed state you are in.

Go through each of the events, picturing them as clearly as if they were repeating themselves now, and hold that feeling too that you experienced at the time.

When you have treated each event on your list, return to the beach (or the forest or meadow if you prefer the country scenes) and remain relaxed for a minute or two before rousing yourself out of this state of relaxation. Don't be in a hurry to get up out of the chair, but savour the delight of that quiet, tranquil moment for a little longer.

In Your New Image

Repeat this exercise for a minimum of three weeks — that magical time your mind needs to accept these pictures of yourself enjoying past pleasures. If possible, try to fit in two sessions (more if you can) just like this one each day. Each one will become easier, the pictures more vivid. The more you think about these past, happy events, the more this feeling will be with you in your daily life, and the better you will see yourself from now on.

At no time during this relaxed visualisation, nor afterwards, should you let undesirable pictures form in your mind. There will be no place in your mind, in your life, for such pictures from now on. Having relived those moments from the past that gave you relief from the otherwise unpleasant and unwelcome pictures you might have become used to, would you even want to contemplate harbouring those undesirable images any more? I sincerely hope not!

Chapter 5 Removing Anxiety

Fear. Anxiety. Which is worse? Which is more restrictive to ourselves, to our lives? It would be hard to say. Perhaps one is really a more intense form of the other? Whatever you say, fear of everyday events — fear of meeting a stranger, fear that you will meet a dog, even a small one, may prevent you from walking down the street. Perhaps dogs are not the only animals you fear.

Maybe you are one of the many people who suffer from a fear of travelling, particularly flying, and transport by water. Fear of boats is quite common. So is a fear of water.

Anxiety too can hold us back from being ourselves more than most of us would like to admit. We feel anxious about those we will have to associate with when we go out. We are anxious that our day might not be a splendid occasion — and how many days are anyway? People become anxious about what others might think about them, the way they dress. They might not like to dress in bright clothing because people might not approve of what they are wearing. I don't do what I would like to because I am afraid that ... Or I would like to attend this or that event, but what would happen ...

Does that all sound far-fetched and unrealistic? I am afraid that none of this is out of the ordinary. People do fear — indeed dread at least some of these events that many others would think of as quite insignificant and of no consequence to themselves whatsoever. But to the sufferers of these inflictions, they are very, very real threats indeed to their wellbeing.

Perhaps you are one of the many who do not like to admit to such personal suffering. Think for a moment how different everyday living would be without threats of these types holding you back, preventing you from being your natural self.

There are a certain number of events we must do in the course of our everyday lives, lest we stagnate and suffocate in our own fear and inactivity. We all have to go outdoors. Most of us have to travel to town, or to work, or at least to the shops to buy our groceries. What sort of relief would it be if we could partake in such events without that nagging fear and anxiety hanging around our necks? I would say that the difference in ourselves, our brighter outlook, the way we feel about ourselves, would be quite remarkable.

WE ALL NEED TO TRAVEL SOMEWHERE, SOMETIME

Most of us have family members who do not live close by us. Travel is essential if we are to see them, even occasionally. Unless, of course, we have understanding relatives who appreciate our feelings and visit us instead. But that does not really help us in the long run. The fear and anxiety are still there.

Visiting our relatives, or the friends we grew up with, is hampered if we fear flying. Flying is a great way to cover vast distances quickly.

Boat travel is another great way to travel to see our friends and loved ones. If, that is, we do not fear boats and, in particular, water.

Being released from such restraints in our personal lives could easily be likened to an outdoors person, chained up for life, suddenly having the padlock undone and the chains released. That person would be free. There would no longer be that chain preventing them from enjoying life, from living.

Removing Anxiety

Are you one of the many people in our societies who is prevented from living as you could? Perhaps prevented from living as you should live?

With fears and anxieties, these conditions develop slowly, perhaps over a period of years, sometimes a couple of decades, ever so slowly creeping up on us. If such a condition were to hit us suddenly, we would notice it and react violently against such a change, and rightly so, too. But if such a condition were to creep up, slowly, slowly inching up in our lives, each progression ever so slowly that the movement was barely discernible, then what? We would not be aware of what was overcoming us. We would not feel it. It would not feel any different to the way we felt yesterday, or perhaps even one week ago.

It is that slow but ever so small progression that will overcome us and, for more people than many of us realise, will mentally cripple us.

How much more exciting would our days be if we could do more, pass every hour of the day in a most fulfilling way? Remove that fear, remove those anxieties, and we are on the way to leading a satisfying and fulfilling life that we might otherwise envy in other people.

Whatever the cause of the fear, whatever the reason behind the anxiety we face in our everyday lives, much of the results can be overcome and removed through simple but effective visualisation. Numerous people have gone about their lives without any notion of what was bothering them weeks earlier ever entering their thoughts. Yet before they visualised such events, they feared every moment. They clearly did not get much out of their lives, no happiness, no pursuits they could say gave them pleasure. Among these were people who shunned society itself for fear of the discomfort and ridicule they thought people would inflict on them. They shunned other people because they were afraid. Afraid of what? There is seldom a clear pattern to the threats in most people's lives, other than perhaps the fear of spiders, and to a much lesser extent the fear of small animals such as mice.

LEARN TO RESPECT SOME FEARS—THEY ARE GOOD FOR US

The fear of spiders is very widespread. Is this a worthwhile fear to be burdened with?

Perhaps it is. Some spiders are dangerous. Some, such as the Australian funnelweb, can give the unsuspecting victim a fatal injection of venom. Other species of spiders are proving to be less of the innocent little critters they were believed to be. Medical knowledge is increasing and is showing that some unknown illnesses, sometimes serious and life-threatening, were caused by 'innocent' spider bites.

And if you completely remove the fear of spiders, be sure you can recognise the dangerous ones. But if you are sensible and reasonable, you should learn to find a compromise between reducing those phobias and fear, sufficient for you to get on with your life without being obsessed by the dangers they impose.

Perhaps a fear of creatures such as spiders is one to respect and not to become too complacent about. Perhaps it might be wise to hold on to at least that fear.

But what about removing those other fears altogether, like the fear of water, or the fear of flying?

There will always need to be some halfway mark to aim for. While we may admire the adventurer who can scale a snow-capped mountain and not feel fear, or climb a rock wall using what looks to the uninitiated rock climber as totally inadequate equipment for the task, these people take calculated risks. They know the dangers, and they respect them.

There is a difference between losing our fear of water and going for a swim on a hot day to cool off and fighting man-eating sharks. That sensible point has to be realised.

Removing Anxiety

There also has to be a sensible point somewhere in between the extremes of flying in a Boeing 747 jet airline, one of the most reliable and safest aeroplanes ever built, and becoming a stunt pilot. While it may be desirable to remove the fear of flying so that we can sit comfortably and peacefully in that jumbo jet, there is no necessity for most of us to take up stunt flying or crop dusting for a bit of stimulation.

The same applies to boating. We can remove the fear of travelling on an inter-island ferry that has made the run several times a day for twenty years without incident, as opposed to taking on gigantic waves on a surf ski.

My suggestion is that if you really would like to remove the anxiety from an event, do so sensibly but not necessarily completely. A fear of an unknown can be a healthy condition. It is what will protect us from ourselves. We weigh up the conditions of the surf, and tell ourselves that the seas are not right for us. Perhaps we can come back another day when they are calm. This fear that we have retained might save us. Respect it, value it. Fear can be inherent for some dangers from the moment we are born. They are our allies to see us through the life ahead.

If only we could each live a normal life, free of those fears that hold us back from being real achievers. If only we could be relaxed about things. If only we could get on with the important things in our lives. If only we didn't worry about every damn thing. If only!

We are reluctant to attend parties because we feel uneasy. We fear rejection by other people. We are afraid that people might treat us coldly, which we take personally as meaning no one wants to talk to us.

We don't go for a promotion in our line of work because it would bring on more responsibility that we fear we won't be able to cope with. We miss out there too.

We don't like examinations, because for the last few we did, we got very poor marks despite the cramming we did for the finals, and despite all that we had put into succeeding. We do not attempt further study, because we would probably do badly at the next examinations too.

Fear truly can be a killer of motivation and success. As I mentioned, fear is very widespread. We all suffer from it in one form or another. The overall effect is that many of us do not reach our true potential in life, in our social standing, in our work, in our studies, in our other achievements.

SOME NEVER GIVE UP

But through the proper use of visualisation, many people have overcome a wide range of fears and have shown that they truly can achieve whatever is the game of life they set out to win. Some have gone from incoherent, bungling blubbers to people who have, only ten days after being introduced to visualisation, given a ten-minute talk to a large class and been congratulated on their clear presentation. With one such case, in his previous talk that was supposed to have lasted only five minutes, the victim of fear of talking was asked to sit down during his presentation because he made such a mess of it! Yet through visualisation, he was able to turn all that around in a very short time. He pictured the desired outcome for himself. He saw himself speaking in a loud, clear and confident tone. In his images he was able to see his audience, look at them, see their eyes looking at him, and, quite unperturbed at this in his images, he rehearsed it over and over in his mind, picturing every last detail of the room, even the blackboard, and the timber panelling behind him.

Incidentally, this same student, after being asked to sit down in his earlier presentation, earned one of the highest marks out of his class of over thirty students for his ten-minute talk. Marks were awarded for clarity, style, method of delivery (use of overheads, use of the blackboard, use of diagrams). Imagine his elation at this sudden turnaround.

Removing Anxiety

Through the use of visualisation in just one part of his life, he was able to lose that fear of public speaking.

Others have, as some would say, simply breezed through difficult interviews, and have won the position in their company that has meant so much to them.

Whatever it is that we overcome, always remember that this is possibly only the beginning. Most people are unlikely to rest there. They are more likely, once they have overcome one obstacle in the game of life, to go on to the next, hurdle over that one, and from there progress through the main handicaps that are holding them back.

Here's how to use visualisation to remove those common anxieties that many of us face in our daily lives to a level where they will no longer hinder us from fully enjoying ourselves.

FEAR OF ANIMALS

For this exercise, we will deal with a small dog, but substitute any other animal that you are likely to encounter regularly and of which you are afraid.

Take a deep breath and let it out slowly, and relax, and count to ten. Picture yourself in a peaceful setting for a minute or two — perhaps sitting in a comfortable chair in your lounge room. You feel happy, calm and relaxed. What does it feel like, to be there? You are at peace with your surroundings. There is nothing at the moment that is bothering you.

See yourself looking through your front window, and seeing a small dog several houses away from you. You realise the animal cannot hurt you because you are in the security of your home while the animal is outside. Watch the dog for a couple of minutes. Is it a long-haired animal? Is it wagging its tail? Is it with someone? Picture the animal clearly.

Now watch it, in your mental picture, as it walks slowly towards your house. It appears to get bigger the closer to you that it gets. You accept that this is quite normal for an object to appear larger the closer it is. Now you see it just outside your front window, but you still feel safe in the security of your own home.

You watch the dog as it sits outside your window, looking in at you. You notice its appealing face, and its attractive markings. You smile at the dog because it wants to come to you. Look at the animal in your mental picture for several minutes. Don't forget there is a lot of protection between you and the dog, and there is a large distance.

Make sure that you are calm and relaxed, free of all muscular tension as you observe the animal in your mind's picture.

Go on observing the dog for a couple more minutes.

Through another's eyes, see yourself getting up and walking slowly towards the door to open it. You look calm and relaxed in this picture. Still through another's eyes, watch as you stand on the front step and look down at the dog. The dog does not approach you, but wags its tail and it looks at you for friendship.

Picture yourself looking at the animal, but feeling relaxed and enjoying this simple experience. Watch the dog from the distance for at least two or three minutes, as the dog in turn looks back at you.

Now, in your mind's picture, call the dog to you. You notice it gets up and walks only slowly towards you, wagging its tail indicating that it is friendly. You are aware that this is a breed of dog that is bred for its good temperament. The dog approaches you, and you remain calm and relaxed. Look at the dog as it sits down by your feet. Watch this scene for several minutes before making any advances to attract the dog any further to you.

Picture yourself bending down and holding out your hand towards it. Remember, you are calm and relaxed, free of all muscular and emotional tension.

Watch, in your mental picture, as the dog accepts your challenge and sniffs your fingers. You hold your hand steady and enjoy this experience. Now see yourself patting the animal gently on its head. The dog, in your picture, responds by simply sitting still and letting you do this.

Now see yourself stroking the dog on the top of its head and down its neck. Again, in the mental picture you are creating, the dog sits there and responds by looking up at you as you make physical contact with it.

See yourself stroking the animal's head and neck for several minutes as the dog merely looks at you, obviously enjoying this experience you are sharing with it.

Through another's eyes, see yourself getting closer to the animal, and putting your other hand on it and running your fingers through the hair on its neck. See yourself doing this for quite a while, remaining calm and relaxed the whole while that you do so.

Now watch the dog as it tires of this and moves away from you and disappears along the street.

Repeat scenes like this with a small dog (or other animal if you prefer) for the first few occasions, gradually increasing the imaginary size of the animal to a reasonable proportion.

OVERCOMING SHYNESS

Take a deep breath and let it out slowly relax, and count to ten. Picture yourself in a peaceful setting for a minute or two.

Picture walking through a shopping arcade. See the people as they walk past you. They are some distance away from you, but the arcade is long and wide, and there is a lot of space between everyone there. Everyone seems to be moving slowly, either strolling along or window shopping. Notice something about each one — what each one is wearing, whether it is an old man, a young woman, a child, a teenager with a couple of friends.

Through another's eyes, notice how you walk, not against the windows of the shopping arcade, but tending to move towards the centre of the concourse. This way, you are nearer

In Your New Image

the people as they pass you, and you can get a better view of them. So notice their faces as they pass you. Are they looking happy? Do they appear sad? Is one smiling? Perhaps one is talking to a companion. Notice their expressions as they go past you.

As you walk along the concourse, the number of people there increases, so they are brought closer together. You are able to get a better look at their faces. Notice the blemishes on their skin, their dimples, whether some are wearing glasses, some might have long hair. Take a look at the faces as each person walks by. You should, throughout this experience of observing the people there, be calm and relaxed, and experiencing no physical tension, particularly in your arms, legs, neck or back muscles. You should not be experiencing any emotional tension either.

Through another's eyes, notice how easy you look with so many people, so many in close proximity to yourself. Watch yourself in this situation for at least several minutes as you continue to walk slowly among the other shoppers.

Go back to sitting comfortably and imagine a small room, just yourself and one other person. Imagine a person you know to be friendly, one who perhaps likes you, and has an outgoing personality. Who is this person? What are they like. How are they dressed today in your picture of them? Where are they sitting? How are they positioned in the room? Form an image that is clear and as real as you can make it.

See yourself in the room, taking part in some activity — sorting cards, cleaning a table, or any other activity that you can think you might be doing in such an event. See the other person across the other side of the room, busy and involved in some activity.

Picture the other person sitting down after the activities and relaxing. In your mental picture, see yourself go up to this person and say hello. Make sure that, as you approach the person in your image, you are feeling quite relaxed, and free from both physical and mental tension. This is important.

Now picture the other person talking to you, and you responding to what has just been said. Imagine that the person has indicated to you to join in some light conversation, an invitation that you accept.

Through another's eyes, see the two of you there, engaged in meaningful conversation. As you watch this scene as if from a distance, notice your face and that of the person you are talking to. Does your face show the true emotion of talking to someone who could become your friend? Are you using your hands to emphasise your point as you speak? And what of the other person—how are they acting at this time? Are they too using their hands a lot as they talk? Make this scene just as vivid as you did with those earlier. Make it like it really would be.

Through another's eyes, watch as the other person asks you to join them for a coffee. Watch as you accept and walk together through the door.

Create numerous scenes in your mind of yourself mixing with other people. Do not force any situation to develop. Keep each encounter with other people in a social context small and simple—for a start, restrict each scene to yourself and perhaps only one or at the most two other people. Then, when you feel confident in the presence of one or two other people, increase the number of people around you in your mental pictures by one more at a time.

Create the pictures as often as you can, as clearly as you can, and make sure that you are completely relaxed, both physically and mentally, in each of these scenes. That sense of relaxation will transfer to the real situation whenever you encounter people who want to talk to you, to include you in their group of friends.

In Your New Image

FEAR OF TRAVELLING

This exercise describes how you can lose the fear of flying, but you should adapt the scenes as appropriate to remove the fear of boating or other forms of transport. The principles are similar.

Take a deep breath, let it out slowly and relax, and count to ten. Picture yourself in a peaceful setting for a minute or two, such as a beach or a meadow.

Now picture yourself relaxing at home, with a planned, but perhaps essential trip that you are dreading, still several days away. Form a clear picture in your mind of packing for your journey, whether it be by ship, or aeroplane, or other means of transport. See yourself taking down that suitcase and wiping the inside with a cloth or a sponge. You are quite relaxed doing this as the picture is only in your own mind. Now see yourself taking some clothes out of your wardrobe and laying them flat on the bed to sort and then to fold. Picture yourself folding the clothes and putting them into the suitcase. Now see yourself closing the lid on the suitcase.

Through another's eyes, watch yourself, still quite relaxed about the proposed journey, carry the suitcase and place it near the door. Notice the relaxed expression on your face as you put the suitcase down beside the door. Now watch as you sit down again in your lounge room.

Develop a mental picture of yourself picking up the tickets to your destination and looking at them. In your mind, read the destination, and put the tickets on a table or a cupboard.

Visualise yourself, while you still feel quite calm and relaxed, pick up the tickets and walk to the door to pick up your suitcase.

Through another's eyes, watch as you open the door with your free hand and close the door after you, pulling it tight as you close up the house before you leave on your trip. Notice how relaxed you look.

Now see yourself waiting out the front of your home for a taxi to arrive to take you to the port, or to the airport to catch

Removing Anxiety

your flight. Watch this scene for several minutes, but make sure that you remain quite calm and relaxed. Make sure that, in your picture, you are not pacing up and down the street or constantly looking at your watch. You should, even in your mind, be calm and relaxed.

In the distance a long way down the road, you see a taxi turn into your street and proceed very slowly towards your home. You realise the vehicle is for you, and you feel excited. Watch the taxi cruise slowly towards you and finally stop.

Through another's eyes, see yourself lifting your suitcase into the taxi and getting in and closing the door. Watch this scene, and especially the one you develop as the taxi takes you towards the port or the airport.

Return to seeing the events through your own eyes. See yourself getting out of the taxi at the airport and proceed through the crowded terminal building towards the check-in counter. You must still be relaxed and quite calm. If you begin to feel nervous at this stage, go back to visualising the last scene you recall in which you were calm. Then let the images in your mind develop forward from that point on.

Imagine yourself looking through the terminal window and noticing a large aeroplane on the tarmac. What airline is it? What colour is it? Are people boarding it at this stage? Make this scene as realistic as you possibly can.

Through another's eyes, see yourself waiting in the lounge at the airport. See all around you the other passengers who will be flying on the same flight as yourself. Look at them. What do you notice about them? What are they wearing? Are they looking happy? Are they excited? Let your mind be as creative as it can be but in a positive way.

Through another's eyes, look at yourself sitting there on the comfortably padded seat in the waiting lounge of the airport for your boarding call. You look calm and relaxed, and your hands are still, folded in your lap. Picture what might be beyond the walls of the terminal. Can you create images of aeroplanes taking off along the runway? Next, imagine yourself getting up on hearing the boarding call, and walking towards the door that leads to the gangway. You still feel calm and relaxed.

Picture yourself getting on board the aeroplane, and being shown your seat by the hostess. Where are you sitting? Are you near the window or near the aisle? Are you near the front of the aeroplane or near the back, or near a wing? Look around you in your mind's picture, as you take in all the sights and sounds of the activity of people getting on board with you. Notice them walking along the aisle past you, and sitting in their seats.

Picture yourself, holding this scene for a good five minutes. You are relaxed, and your mind is calm and free of all tension. You are still, your muscles, particularly those in your arms and legs, neck and back, are without tension.

See in your mind the aeroplane pulling out from the terminal and proceeding slowly to the end of the runway. How does this feel? Are you paying attention to the precautionary safety instructions? Are you looking out of the window at the activity outside? Picture this movement clearly. Remember, the aeroplane at this stage will be taxiing very slowly to the end of the runway, so you can be quite relaxed about the movement.

Through another's eyes, watch yourself sitting in the seat, looking out of the aeroplane as it remains stationary at the end of the runway waiting for clearance to take off. Picture this moment for several minutes. Remember, the aeroplane is not moving, it is waiting for clearance. Now see yourself sitting, quite calm and relaxed, as the aeroplane speeds along the runway and becomes airborne.

Through another's eyes, see yourself sitting back, relaxed in your seat, drinking a cup of coffee that the hostess has brought you. See yourself enjoying this cup of coffee, and looking out of the window as you fly high over the ground.

Practise scenes like these for as long a time as you have available before your flight, and the actual event will not be at all traumatic to you. Rather, it will become quite a pleasurable experience.

FEELING RELAXED AND COMFORTABLE WITH THE OPPOSITE SEX

Take a deep breath, let it out slowly and relax, and count to ten. Picture yourself in a peaceful setting for a minute or two such as on a beach or other tranquil place.

Now picture yourself sitting on a comfortable chair, quite relaxed, perhaps looking around you at the faces of the other people in a room with you. The setting could be at a party or some other social engagement that your friends have asked you to attend.

Study the faces for some time, picturing first one, then looking to the next, studying that, before looking at the next face in the room.

Make sure that you are quite relaxed, both physically and mentally, as this is important as the sense of relaxation transfers to the real situation that will follow.

Through another's eyes, see yourself looking around you, taking a good look at those in the room with you. The number of individuals has increased considerably by now. See yourself looking towards the door, and notice more people arriving. What is the atmosphere of the room like? Is it well lit? Is it dim? Are there tables around the walls, perhaps with food on them? Picture the setting very clearly, as if you were in that room, attending the social event.

See yourself looking at more faces of the people who have just come in. One person of the opposite sex stands out. The person is about your age, and you would like to talk to that person.

What does this person look like? Is the person your height? Your build, or thinner or perhaps a little heavier than you are?

Is the person's hair dark or fair? Does the person wear glasses, or bright clothes, or is there anything else that stands out?

You feel that you would very much like to get to meet that person, start up a conversation, and extend an invitation to dinner.

Through another's eyes, see yourself sitting in that chair as the person slowly comes towards you. You look calm and relaxed, but excited because you have the opportunity to get a better look at them. You see yourself with your eyes on them as they get nearer and nearer to you. How is this person walking? Are they smiling? Are they looking around the room as they approach your chair?

Now see yourself in your picture as the person stands right beside you. Hold that picture of the person by your side for about three or four minutes. You feel relaxed, but emotionally excited, but you are free of muscular tension. Emotional feelings are acceptable in situations like this, otherwise your personality would be as flat as a piece of paper. But the muscles of your legs, back, arms and neck during this scene should be quite relaxed.

Observe that person. How are they standing? Are their arms folded, or straight down their sides? Are they standing erect, or slouching or leaning? Are they looking out across the room, or talking to another person?

In your mental picture you have formed of the person, see them slowly turn towards you and say hello.

Through another's eyes, see yourself smile warmly, and in a calm, confident voice, reply to their greeting. Do not rush this scene at all in your image. Let this stage develop slowly and carefully. If you find you are tending to rush the scene, or feel physical tension, go back to visualising the last scene during which you felt relaxed.

Picture yourself sitting down with the person beside you, both turned towards one another, talking. Sense what this would feel like to you. Notice the person's eyes, hair and clothes as you are having this conversation.

Removing Anxiety

Hold this scene of the two of you in convivial conversation for about five minutes or longer. Again, I should stress that you must not rush this event, but let it unfold slowly and naturally.

Through another's eyes, watch as you (or the other person) suggest you both have a drink. This is time to redevelop your relaxation and ensure that you are not physically tense.

Now see the two of you sitting closer to each other, over a social drink. You both feel relaxed and happy. See yourself listening to their conversation, enjoying what they are saying. You should be able to almost hear the conversation you are having with this person. Notice their gestures as they speak. Be aware of your own gestures, part of 'body language' as you engage in interesting conversation. Hold this scene for a good ten minutes — longer if you can.

Through another's eyes, watch the two of you engaged in mutually satisfying conversation, obviously enjoying each other's company.

Make sure you feel very relaxed and calm. In your image, turn to the other person, and simply extend an invitation to go out to dinner with you next weekend. Feel good about asking this question.

Visualise scenes such as these for a while before social events, and notice the difference in your social life!

PREPARING FOR EXAMINATIONS

Take a deep breath, let it out slowly and relax, and count to ten. Picture yourself getting ready for that important examination. Picture yourself, days, if not weeks before that examination, dressing in your casual clothes that you will be comfortable wearing. See yourself checking that you have your pens in your pocket and other materials you are allowed — calculator, any notes that you will be permitted to take in with you.

Now picture yourself stepping outside. Did you hear the door close? Hear the latch click behind you, really hear it. You

In Your New Image

are relaxed. Look at yourself through someone else's eyes, you are strolling out of the house, calm, self assured, comfortable. You feel good about the day. Picture that morning, feel the air, make it as vivid as you can.

Imagine yourself heading off to the examination room. Get a clear picture in your mind of what it might look like—a small room, or a huge hall. See the other students there. How many of them are there in that room where you will be? Picture yourself arriving, meeting fellow students that you know. See yourself greeting your friends, exchanging light-hearted conversation. But see yourself, around all the other people, remaining calm and as comfortable as though you are going on holidays. Feel those muscles—they are very relaxed, there's no tension in them at all. Your mind feels good and clear, and you feel no concern at all about the next two or three hours. You are actually looking forward to the examination, so feel this emotion, feel what it is like to be there, relaxed in the knowledge that you know all you could have learned for this examination. You remain calm and relaxed.

Picture yourself looking at the door of the examination room. What does it look like? And the room behind it, what is that like? Picture what you think it will be like. How high are the ceilings? What colours are the walls? See them, see the marks on the paintwork, see the windows in the room. How many are there? Are they high in the walls, or normal height? Form the clearest mental picture of the examination room that you can.

Now picture yourself walking confidently through that door to find your desk. Look around you in your picture. Where are the other students sitting? Are there many in front of you? Either side of you? Put more and more students into your picture. See them. Hear the noise of their voices and footsteps as they look for their places.

See yourself in your mind sitting down at your place. Look at the other students, and the activities occurring all around you. You feel calm and relaxed still, not at all tense or nervous.

Removing Anxiety

Look down at your desk. There are a couple of pieces of paper on the desk in front of you. They do not alarm you. You take this sight into your grasp and accept it as just part of the examination process. Still feeling calm and relaxed, you look carefully at one piece of paper. You know that that one is the examination paper itself, and you feel excited about turning it over and reading it. You feel good at this stage because you know you have studied and learnt all you could have, and prepared yourself well for this day.

Now feel the room, hear it go quiet. See the people all around you, sitting, quietly, in anticipation. Feel the mood. Feel relaxed. See yourself there at your desk, actually realising that your limbs are not at all tense, your neck is relaxed, and your forehead is smooth and not tense.

Look at yourself again through someone else's eyes. See yourself sitting there in anticipation of being granted permission to turn the examination paper over. Hold that feeling of relaxed anticipation for several minutes.

The whole scene for you, as you can see yourself, is one of calm, feeling good about yourself, wanting to get on with the job of expressing your thoughts and writing down your answers.

Hear in your mind the voice that tells you to turn the examination paper over and read through it. Picture your delight at reading through the questions, feeling that elation as you pass from one question to the next one.

Picture yourself beginning to write the answers, referring several times to the question paper. What are you writing with? What sort of pen? What colour is it? What does the desk look like? Is it small or wide? Is it clean and new, or old and badly marked?

See yourself through someone else's eyes writing and writing, turning over the pages in your answer book.

Imagine yourself finishing one question and beginning to write the next one. See the words appearing on that page in front of you. Just picture everything in absolute detail, just as if you were actually there at that examination.

You are nearing the end of that examination, so picture yourself finishing the last question with only a few minutes to go, and reading through your answers. You can feel good that you have given the answers that you have written. You feel good because you know beyond doubt that you have passed with a very high mark.

Think passing. Picture yourself passing that examination. Feel good about being there, writing all the right answers.

Distance yourself from that imaginary examination and see yourself reading your results, either on a sheet you have received in the mail, or on the institution's notice board. See yourself mentally jumping with joy as you see the high mark you were awarded for your efforts.

See yourself as a successful student. You will be.

PUBLIC SPEAKING

Take a deep breath, let it out slowly, relax, and count to ten. Picture yourself in a peaceful setting for a minute or two — a forest or meadow or walking along the beach.

Picture yourself an hour or so before you would have to make your speech. Where will you be addressing your audience? Is it in the building you know well? What does that building look like? What is your topic going to be?

Picture clearly in your mind the room where you will be talking to your audience. Is it big or small? Is it brightly lit? Are there windows all along the wall? Where is the door? Is it a long narrow room or a square or rectangular one? See it as clearly as it is possible to get a picture in your mind.

Through another's eyes, see yourself alone in the front of the room standing at the lectern. You look relaxed, at ease with yourself, and are waiting for the people to come through the door.

Removing Anxiety

Watch this person—yourself—for a couple of minutes or more.

See the room again through your own eyes. Look around you in your picture. You feel relaxed and enthusiastic. You feel calm about the talk—this is essential, because the feeling of calmness you are experiencing in this image will transfer itself to the real situation when you are required to talk in public to a large audience.

Look at the door of the auditorium or room. You notice someone enter at the far end of the room. You smile, and watch the person sit down in the middle of the room.

Observe this person for a short time, feeling that sense of relaxation and tranquility you now experience.

Now look at the far end of the room and watch another person come into the room slowly and sit down.

You still enjoy that calm and relaxed experience.

Through another's eyes, see yourself in the front of the room standing at the lectern, looking at your notes. See yourself looking down and checking that they are in order.

See your notes now from your own perspective. Can you see the writing on the sheets of paper? Can you see the diagrams you have prepared? They should be clear in the image you are holding of yourself. Look up and watch a couple more people come into the room. You should still feel relaxed and accept that you are going to get a good number of people to hear you speak.

Spend about ten minutes while remaining calm and relaxed, watching the people enter the room, one at a time, and go to their seats. (It is easier to accept a small increase over a longer time than it is to see a tide of people washing into the auditorium). So watch them, and see yourself through another's eyes as you stand in front of the audience, calm and relaxed, waiting for the last one to enter and close the door.

It will soon be time to begin your talk. You know you will be introduced to the audience, so see yourself going to a seat near the front of the room and sitting down, facing the audience.

Is the audience talking? Are they lively? Are they smiling and laughing with one another?

See all the people — one at a time if you wish. Make them real. Make them all different. Put into your mental picture people you recognise. Put in others who are your peers and your colleagues.

See the person who will introduce you to your audience approach you and speak to you. Through another's eyes, watch as you respond. What scene do you notice? Are you calm? Are you confident?

Watch the person introduce you. You listen to comments about yourself, and why you have been chosen to give the talk, and what your purpose will be on this occasion.

Through another's eyes, see yourself rise, slowly and confidently, and walk to the lectern. See yourself standing in front of your audience, adjusting your notes, and looking up at the audience.

Now look at the audience through your own eyes. Stand there, feeling relaxed and calm as you look around the room. Are the people there looking at you? Are any of the seats in the room empty? Have the lights dimmed or is the room brightly lit? This scene must look realistic as you see it in your mind. Listen to the sounds in your mind — the occasional cough, the movement of someone's foot all add to the realism of the scene.

See yourself take a deep breath as you begin to talk to your audience. You speak with a loud and confident voice — a voice that reflects your expertise in your subject, and one that conveys your dynamic approach to the talk. Feel the enthusiasm as you see yourself talking to your audience. Feel the mood in the room. Listen. Feel the warmth or the coolness of the air.

Picture yourself, using that same clear, loud voice, conveying your message. Hear the tone of your voice, feel yourself delivering your presentation to that audience.

Your audience on this occasion was not real, so you have many, many chances to perfect your talk to audiences both large

Removing Anxiety

and small. Repeat your delivery many times. See your delivery of your talk in large rooms in front of large audiences. See yourself talking to small groups in small rooms. See it often, because your mind will accept those images of you giving the confident presentation you have created and return the same dynamic style when you face the real audience to deliver a talk. Your mind, if you rehearse the scenes often enough, will not be able to tell the difference between those people you have created, and the audience that is there in front of you.

And, like most skills, your speech will become more interesting, your presentation more dynamic, the more you rehearse the public speaking.

Chapter 6 Accepting Ourselves

The trouble with aging is that we change—not behaviourally, but physically. We generally tend to grow plumper unless we watch our weight carefully. Most of that excess weight that we don't like ourselves for is partly due to a slowing down in physical activities while maintaining around the same number of calories consumed each day. Excess calories consumed, plus reduced burning of calories, must equal weight gain.

But other parts of our bodies change with time too. We (males especially) lose some or much of our hair. Our eyes change and we find it difficult to read close up. The result—we begin wearing glasses that we have dreaded wearing for the first fifty years of our lives.

Not all the things we tend to dislike about ourselves develop late in life. Height is another characteristic that seldom pleases many people. There is, I suppose, an average height. There has to be such a term if we measure a certain number of people and divide their total heights by the number of individuals we have measured.

But how many people are exactly that 'average' height? Perhaps not as many as one might suppose, for to get any average, there must be a wide range of measurements that, evened out, will give us that figure that we call average.

Whether we are about average, above average height (taller), or are a long way from that middle figure, many people are not satisfied with their height. Yet height, probably more than any other physical quality, is the one we can do least about other than accept it.

A lot of people go through life with a distorted personality merely because they cannot accept how short or tall they are. Yet self acceptance of ourselves, as we have seen elsewhere in this book, is more fundamental to a happy disposition and pleasant personality and bright outlook on life than just about any other aspect we are likely to encounter during our progression through life. We might as well accept ourselves as we are and get on with living. There's not much else we can do about a lot of things, so why bother, other than to accept ourselves?

Weight is another physical feature that many people do not like about themselves. While a thinner person (and I do not mean those who look like a bag of bones) feels better and has more energy and can do more physical activities and is, generally, in better health than one who is considered 'above average' in weight, acceptance of our weight is less expensive than the money that would otherwise be paid out by individuals for diets, weight reduction programs, training programs, and numerous other time-consuming activities that seldom work long term and collectively cost individuals of countries billions of dollars every year.

HOW BIG ARE YOU? IT'S ALL IN YOUR MIND

Weight gain, as I have pointed out, is usually (but there are exceptions) due to an excess intake of calories compared with the number of calories we burn in physical work, or simply use in the process of staying alive. Diets usually fail, even if we get short-term benefits from the occasional diet that promises hope to those enduring it. There is evidence that dieting damages your health. Over time, though, the diet will fail in over ninety percent of people. It it not necessarily because they have weakened their will and have gone back to raising their intake of food, but because the human body (and those of most other animals) prepares for another pending shortage of food in its expectations of a harsh period ahead. That is our body's natural reaction to finding itself in a situation of food shortage. The body's metabolism will tick along at a much slower rate, so we will need far fewer calories to make it tick over than we did before the diet. That's the way the body works in its natural environment. It is a means to ensuring its survival during times of severe food shortage. And that is something we now have to live with. One solution though to reducing some excess weight is to burn more calories through increased output of energy. The basal metabolic rate rises about ten to fifteen percent for twelve hours after only thirty minutes or more of exercise. Therefore, if we exercise for one hour a day over two shorter periods, we will raise our basal metabolic rate by fifteen percent over the whole day.

Weight loss can be safely achieved by this means, even by maintaining the same intake of calories. But this chapter is about accepting our weight (if we are not interested in genuinely and permanently reducing the fat).

One word of warning is necessary here. There are two food-related illnesses associated with our images of weight. Anorexia nervosa is where people see themselves constantly as being too fat, and will, despite their underweight and poor nourishment, nevertheless try as hard as they can to lose more weight — simply because they see themselves as too fat.

The other is a related disorder, bulimia nervosa, where people eat and eat but purge themselves of food. Clearly, both groups of people have a severe problem with an incorrect mental image of themselves.

The aim of talking about weight here, is not to change your weight, but to accept yourself just as you are. Think carefully about the difference. Do not under any circumstance, unless guided carefully by a practitioner who is experienced in this field, see yourself as a weight you are not.

Accepting Ourselves

Instead of spending decades thinking we are too thin, too fat, too short or too tall, visualisation provides all of us with a powerful tool that will allow us to get on with what really is important in the game of life. And like all games, that of living should be fun too.

So why should we let our height get us down. Why should we let our weight get us down? And why should we let those other features that are inevitable, get us down. It is, I believe, far easier to accept them than to change them.

YOU MUST FEEL GOOD ABOUT YOURSELF

I appreciate that it is most people's dream to look their best to other people, and to themselves. But one must ask if the pain, the suffering, the anxiety and cost of cosmetic surgery are warranted. Such measures work (but not always), but their gain is beneficial only until the next stage of aging creeps up on the individual. Five or so years after the operations that have given such people a slightly younger look, they are back again to look younger than they really are. Is all this worth it? Is it justified? Many would say not, others would disagree. Although that is a decision a person will have to make as an individual, the alternative is to be our age, literally, and age gracefully with the times. If we are fifty years old, then is there anything wrong with looking like a fifty-year-old man or woman? If we are sixty years old, again, what is wrong with that? We are, well, sixty years old, and that is about all there is to the matter. To quote what just about all of us were told when we were small children ... act your age!

Can you act your age? Of course you can. You can see yourself as you are, and accept yourself just like you are, through visualisation.

Below is an example of how you can achieve self acceptance in these factors through visualisation, and feel really good about yourself.

In Your New Image

ACCEPTING YOURSELF AS YOU ARE
Take a deep breath, let it out slowly and relax, and count to ten. Picture yourself in a peaceful setting for a minute or two — on the beach, for example.

Now see yourself in a picture in your mind, your real self — short, tall, plump, wearing spectacles, thinning around the hair line.

Hold that image of the real you for at least a few minutes. In your picture, study each one of your features in turn. Look at them, scrutinise them, and see these features as part of the real you. As you picture each one in turn, feel yourself smiling in acceptance that that feature is part of the whole of you, your individualism, your character.

If you are aware that your hair is thinning, focus on this for a moment or two, and accept that your hair is thinning, but you look quite all right like that.

Now, in your mind's picture, see yourself looking in a mirror and see yourself wearing spectacles. You have chosen them carefully, and know that they look fine on your face. If in your mental picture you realise that they really don't suit your face — the colour of your skin, the shape of your face, or they are too prominent — then you could seriously consider choosing a pair that is more appropriate to your physical features and your complexion.

But assuming the spectacles do suit your features, hold that picture of yourself wearing them in your mind for a couple of minutes, accepting that this is really you, you don't mind them at all, indeed, they even make you look more distinguished, as many people who wear spectacles have found to their credit and pleasure.

Now see yourself looking in that mirror again. Make no judgment, other than to see yourself as you really are, and as you look at yourself, feel good about yourself. Hold that picture of yourself for at least a couple of minutes, but make sure that you feel positive about what you feel. If your first reaction is to

Accepting Ourselves

say 'yuck', it is time either to picture something else or come back to seeing yourself as you are at a time when you can be either indifferent or preferably positive about the way you look.

Through another's eyes, see yourself sitting on a chair, your hair thinning, wearing spectacles. See yourself, and realise that you look really good after all. Hold this picture of yourself for a couple of minutes. Now study each of your features in turn, accepting that each one is part of you, and that it looks or feels good.

Now picture yourself again as you really are. Go through each of these visions of your individual features one by one, each time accepting them with a most positive feeling.

Over only a short period, if you hold these types of pictures of yourself clearly and for long enough with the right positive attitude and feeling, you will accept yourself as you really are and get on with the more important things in your life that you would really like to do.

Chapter 7 Dealing With Difficult People

There is one good thing about the friends that we have. We enjoy their companionship, their stimulation, and we derive pleasure from doing things with them. We clearly pick friends that we like.

It is unfortunate that we do not pick our relatives. We inherit them, whether we like them or not. We select our partner, of course. If that person has been in a relationship before and has children from that relationship, then we do not necessarily pick those children.

And like those relatives who, unlike our well-chosen friends, give us little companionship and stimulation, so too with our work companions. If we are the employer in a firm, then we do have some say as to whom we select to work with us. But even then, on reflection we find there are people we would have preferred not to have employed. Most employees have little or no say as to whom they will work with.

Often we work with people we just don't like. It might be their mannerisms that we abhor. It might be a personality clash — two people who are quite mismatched for one another. They might be people whom we can find nothing good to say about them. Perhaps this is painting a dim picture of the worst case of workmates. But just about every firm has someone, in some office or department, that someone, some people, do not like. Yes, we tolerate them in the name of keeping the peace, but that is not the same as liking them.

Dealing With Difficult People

If we work with, or for some other reason feel we need to associate with people of this category, then we are faced with two options. The first is to change our circumstances. Clearly for most of us, that is not always a viable option at all. Not many of us will dispense with our partner merely because we do not like their father or sister. We don't get rid of a good husband because he has a brother who is a slob who tries to antagonise those who have the misfortune to come too close to him. We don't normally dispose of a fantastically lovely wife simply because her mother is a busybody who can't stop talking from breakfast time to supper the following day. No, in these circumstances, it is more appropriate, and far more sensible, to practise avoidance wherever possible.

Even at clubs, we have the option of not going out. We can avoid going to social functions (unless they are seen to be essential for our career success).

Perhaps the only time under normal circumstances where we find we must tolerate the intolerable, is at work.

We may work with terrific people and can't find enough time to spend with them. You might, as a group, not only work together, but be a bunch of friends outside work. That's great. But most readers would have encountered the other end of the scale.

A harmonious working environment is essential for productivity and the wellbeing of all workers. The harmony within the working environment will ensure that work is performed to a very high standard. So, for the sake of that mythical being called harmony, we keep quiet. We don't roar at them like we feel we really should. We make sure that we don't say the wrong thing on Monday mornings that we know will start them off on the wrong track for the rest of the week. We pent up our anger and emotions for the sake of peace.

To make the work situation worse, there are managers who take the side of the antagonist, precluding any of the staff who have genuine grievances regarding their colleagues from expressing their concerns. And so the pent-up emotions escalate even further.

Often it is that pent-up emotion and anger that is the cause of even greater anger and intolerance.

It is that pent-up anger that will get us fiery tempered at home. It is our unexpressed feelings that we take home and unleash on our innocent partners or children. And therein lies a greater cause of disharmony than the one we have prevented from happening at work.

TOLERANCE IS BETTER THAN ANGER

For many, they cannot win in such intolerable situations.

It will surprise many readers to learn that acceptance of such people can effectively be controlled by visualisation.

This is not to say that the obnoxious person will go away. It is not for a moment suggesting that the vile person is going to change. It is not to suggest that the perceived villain is going to look at himself and realise the folly of his behaviour and attitude, and turn himself into a model citizen. That is asking for the impossible to become the reality. It won't happen. It never will.

But, with visualisation, it is relatively easy to change the way we see that person who causes the unpleasantness, and so change our reaction to them. Remember, to change the world, it is far easier and simpler merely to change ourselves.

And that is what visualisation can and will do in the cause of a harmonious work environment (or any other environment where we encounter people whom we would prefer not to add to our list of best friends).

With visualisation, we see ourselves as quite relaxed in the company of that person. We see them in our mind as being close by us but without our normal reaction to their presence.

Dealing With Difficult People

We see ourselves talking to that person without wanting to scream. We can even see ourselves cooperating with that person and being productive together.

Try to look at why that person might be the cause of much anguish to you. If it is just that you feel this way about a certain person, then it might be that the person evokes a reaction — he or she might remind you of someone who caused you much pain and concern many years earlier. You might even be able to identify the cause of this antagonism, and resolve the difficulties between the two of you peacefully.

Or perhaps he is a person who upsets the entire office or factory. In that case, it is more likely that the cause of the anguish is that person, not all the workers individually.

Bear in mind that that person might behave that way for one of several reasons. Maybe looking for companionship — as strange as this idea might sound at first, that person will know that he or she will at least get some attention.

But there are rewards for working cooperatively with such a person. They will respond to you and to the different attitude you express towards them. Almost without exception, that person will likewise treat you differently. You will quite likely find that they no longer try to antagonise you. Having said that, I will be the first to admit that there are people who do not respond in the normal way. They think they can justify their actions and behaviour. Unfortunately, it is unlikely that responding to them better will make them any more amenable. Accept them as they are then, and make the most of the situation. But nevertheless, changing your attitude and the way you react to them, will make life tolerable and far more joyous for yourself. Don't kill your spirit through anger. Make the most of the situation.

Your working companions will appreciate you more. Your home life will be without those frustrations and the unpleasantness you encounter during your working life (and remember, often our feelings to such a person, to such a situation, carry through to after we leave work). They haunt us over the weekends, and during the evening when we should be able to dissociate ourselves from our work and distance ourselves from such situations.

If, after you have sincerely — and I emphasise sincerely — done all the exercises in this book that are appropriate to you, there might be one shackle that is beyond your control. It could simply be termed 'other people'.

There are other people — 'managers' — who tell their staff they are stupid. There are 'managers' who tell and show their staff they are incompetent. Even to staff who do a damn good day's work and do it well, these 'managers' will still say they haven't done it properly. These aren't really managers. They are little people with very severe inferiority complexes who make themselves feel better even though they feel bad themselves. They make themselves feel better by believing — and many do believe it — that those around them are worse off.

If you pull one of these people to pieces — do it mentally — it will help you see what makes them work. You may find that they lack skills themselves. They certainly lack the personality qualities that are going to make them popular — a sense of humour, good conversationalist at parties. You may have the misfortune to be married to a spouse or partner who, no matter how hard you try to please them, they will simply tell you that you are silly, that you are a useless person.

I once had a boss whose favourite saying began with the words 'in a perfect world ...' Well, in a perfect world, most bosses are predictable. Unfortunately, there are some, and I have experienced them probably as much as you have, whose behaviour is erratic, unpredictable and irresponsible.

In the perfect world, with relaxation techniques described throughout this book, visualisation such as that I have just described can remove the imagined intimidation and imagined or otherwise threats effectively and in a very short time.

Dealing With Difficult People

Unfortunately we do not live in a perfect world, and some time we will meet those unpredictable bosses. You will overcome the nervousness or other reaction you have just rid yourself of. The next day your boss will try some other form of nerve-wracking antic. You will overcome that characteristic with visualisation. He then will change his spots and you will be inflicted with yet another form of intimidating or destructive, insulting behaviour. It is indeed unfortunate that there are managers, or more correctly, mismanagers of this type running organisations or departments within larger organisations. With the confidence you will gain by performing the techniques described in this book, perhaps the only way to get around these mismanagers is to develop the courage (and you will see how you can) to find another place of employment.

Unfortunately, it is going to be hard overcoming the negativism of these people. I'll say persevere with the mismanager, you can change jobs if they are available, or you can branch out on your own.

With your partner though, for a number of reasons — loyalty, love, circumstances, children — it isn't always easy to overcome. However, don't give up, you will have the confidence after reading this book to handle them in a logical way.

Chapter 8 Acquiring New Skills

Research has shown us over recent years that just imagining ourselves doing something will evoke the same physiological response as the actual event will produce in our bodies. That means that the muscles and the neurons will respond equally to both the visual cue (the image we create of ourselves doing something), and the actual event.

Does this mean, then, that if we merely picture ourselves running, cycling, swinging a golf club, then we will improve our performance?

It may seem strange, but the positive answer is, as I mentioned, borne out by research beyond doubt.

But at the outset I should explain that we won't be able to develop the full muscle density in our limbs simply by picturing ourselves running a marathon. Visualisation will however help us gain at least a considerable increase in muscle bulk. For full muscle bulk development to occur, we do need that physical activity. But the picture that we create of ourselves doing something, such as running, jumping or cycling, will improve our performance as if we had practised and practised extensively. Did you get that? Let me repeat it—the imaging that we create of ourselves doing something will improve our performance as if we had practised and practised extensively. Even if we do nothing for a week or ten days other than to picture ourselves participating in such events, the results will be

Acquiring New Skills

about the same as if we had been out every day for an hour or more, practising our preferred activity.

When I was at school, I did not enjoy sports. I would always much prefer to read an interesting book, or walk in a park looking at the insects or birds. Despite months and months of tennis coaching, my performance did not improve. If it had been physically possible, I would swear that on occasions it actually deteriorated because of the practice.

I was sent to tennis coaching two mornings a week before school — a total waste of my parents' money, but at the time I did not know any better.

And despite a real effort every week after school and on weekends to improve my tennis performance, the coach would admonish me for not having practised. He would never accept my argument that I had really given it my best. There was no point in continuing the argument, because he could see for himself that I did not improve from week to week. Anyway, what else was he to believe?

But one week, I pictured myself hitting the ball, just as he had shown me how to. I pictured it in slow motion coming at my racquet from different angles. I saw the ball coming at me from high up, and in my mind I would study the trajectory of the ball, plan my shot and hit it. The ball went exactly where I had planned for it to go, because I was taking care to play tennis properly in my mind.

And during my lessons, I would hit the tennis ball over the net, at my imaginary opponent, to the coach, then over the net again.

I dreaded the next coaching session on the following Tuesday, because other more interesting activities had absorbed me for all my spare time. I wasn't even aware of where I had left my racquet.

But in real life, that did not matter, for on that next Tuesday morning, the coach praised me up on numerous times for really getting stuck into it. It was a credit to me, he told he. He was proud of my performance.

But in reality, had I practised? In my mind, yes, and that brought on the tremendous change in performance.

Would physical practice have worked better? With my tennis, no. Practice—and I mean probably ten or twelve hours a week—made no improvement at all. But one week's visualisation of improved performance, well, that was different. That achieved real results whereas weeks, numerous hours of real practice had failed.

BE A WINNING SPORTS PERSON

And so it can be with just about any activity, such as running, or playing golf.

With golf, most people complain that they cannot spare the time to get out as much as they should on the greens to improve their round in their favourite game. But ... who really lacks the time to imagine themselves playing? It would be difficult to find more than a very small number who are so busy that they genuinely cannot afford the time to play golf in their minds. Even a few minutes at a time will give them that edge over their opponents.

With activities such as golf, the player knows basically what is required of them. They know how to select the right club, how to hold it, how to swing and follow through after they have hit the ball. And in visualising the desired result—improving their round of golf—it is only the basic skill that is required to begin with. One does not, in the early stages, need to be a professional golf player to benefit from visualisation.

Most people would correctly appreciate that playing well enhances their enjoyment of the game. So, to play well, picture the desired result—see yourself playing like a professional golfer, and you will.

Acquiring New Skills

But physiological improvements too, like endurance, extending your distance as a runner, or as a cyclist, or racing faster, are achievable through the simple technique of visualisation. Don't forget that research has backed up this statement and shown that our bodies react in just the same way as if we were practising our event.

Imagine wanting to improve our speed as a runner. Is that possible? It is a matter of seeing ourselves performing at our best in our minds, and then, still in that mental picture of ourselves performing, see ourselves giving our performance a burst of strength or speed and holding it. We don't want to double our distance or speed overnight. Let the mind adapt to the body's improved speed. Let it adapt to what it can do, accept its output as real. Then it is time to give it another boost in speed or output. That boost we visualise will, over a short time, be demonstrated in our physical output or performance. How? Simply because we have seen ourselves performing better than we thought we could, allowing the mind sufficient time for it to accept that as fact. The mind will over time accept just about any image we create and accept it as fact. Improved performance and output will become fact.

DON'T TRY TO EXCEED THE LIMITS

Bear in mind the limits. Physically, people are able to run at around twenty-five kilometres an hour maximum. Our bodies simply cannot go any faster. To aim for a speed of thirty kilometres an hour would be ridiculous.

We can notice the same improvements through visualising ourselves increasing our endurance in any performance that taxes our physical limits. Don't run a marathon in your mind if you cannot run one hundred metres. The mind won't accept that as fact for quite a while. But see yourself instead running one hundred and fifty metres until that distance is comfortable (combined with physical training for that distance). Once you can handle that distance comfortably, see yourself running two hundred, then three hundred and four hundred metres at a time, and at your fastest speed.

Build up your performance just as you would in actual training.

Think about how you can improve your hobbies. As much as we enjoy pastimes such as carpentry, cooking, sewing, artistic metalwork or whatever it is that gives us rewards of a non-monetary kind, the time we devote to such events is seldom enough because of other necessary commitments of time.

But that does not mean that, in our spare moments — five, ten minutes during the morning, ten minutes while we drink a cup of coffee, or just before going to sleep each evening — that we don't have time to improve our skills.

You will know the basic skills needed for any such hobby or pastime, because you will have already performed all the tasks numerous times to at least have got you interested. Once you have acquired those basic skills, then visualising yourself doing those skills will certainly improve your performance about as much as if you were, say, working in your carpentry shed for hours on end.

Try building a whole table, or a bookshelf in your mind. Go through every step. Picturing yourself building a table or a bookshelf is not unreasonable — many people do it already when they start a project. Unfortunately, most people only build a small portion of the item and leave the rest unfinished.

If you are interested in welding, and many people are, then see yourself constructing a fancy wrought-iron gate for your driveway. See yourself measuring the steel, cutting the lengths, laying them out where each will go. See yourself constructing the scrolls, and welding them into position. Build it in your mind first to avoid costly mistakes.

A friend of mine some years ago, with few woodworking skills, wanted to build himself a row boat. At my suggestion, he built the boat several times in his mind before he even started

Acquiring New Skills

cutting the wood. The result may not have been professional, but it was a credit to someone who, only weeks earlier, did not possess a saw or a screw driver! Yet a simple footstool that he built after he had finished and launched the boat, was less than professional. The difference was that he had not visualised himself building the second item. The result, on this occasion, never made it into his house!

Is there a limit then, as to what skills can be developed by using visualisation? Perhaps not.

MOST IMPROVEMENTS ARE POSSIBLE

Just about all jobs these days require typing—or as it is now known, keyboard skills. I have seen amazing results in improving keyboard skills by older two-finger typists. They never graduated to full touch typing status, but nevertheless they improved from slow, two-finger typists to people who could type at between fifty and sixty words a minute, virtually error free. Such improvements were generally attainable by ordinary people in only three or four weeks of practice, typing in every spare moment—in their minds.

And improving reading speed is easily attainable too by picturing ourselves reading at a slightly faster rate each time. Again, one should not aim for increases of five hundred percent in one day. But gradual improvements in both speed and comprehension are easily attainable by just about anyone willing to devote time to achieving desired improvements.

Often an argument against improving typing speed, or reading speed is that it takes too long. It might take three or four weeks, with numerous short, some long, sessions, picturing such activities. But the counter argument to this is that the time wasted in not improving speed in such skills will, over a lifetime, waste a lot more time, just in lost productivity and frustration.

In Your New Image

But that time argument in any development is meaningless. It merely shows that putting up such weak arguments is no more than an excuse. If we are leaving to go overseas on holidays in six weeks time, then the time will pass quickly. If we are looking forward to seeing a game in four weeks time and have already bought the tickets, then that time will soon pass. The same can be said of attaining improvements in any endeavour through visualisation. Those four weeks are just as long — or short — a time period as that spent waiting for the game, or waiting for your plane to fly out.

Many of us limit ourselves, either deliberately or unintentionally. Some people have the attitude that 'I can only walk ten kilometres.' How do they know? They don't, because they have never been further.

But suppose someone genuinely could walk only ten kilometres, but needed to walk further. How can visualisation help them? It's simple. They imagine themselves walking further. They see themselves walking on their ten-kilometre route. But then they see themselves walking their regular route, but next time, they put in a diversion that will add a small amount — perhaps a couple of kilometres or so. They walk that distance a few times — at least picture themselves walking, or as some who are familiar with the powerful effects of visualisation would say, it's the same thing! Then they see themselves walking their regular twelve-kilometre trip a few times, but then they add another diversion. Soon they are able to walk fifteen kilometres in their images, and in reality they will be able to walk a similar distance. I know that many readers are going to say that this is just wishful thinking. That's in some ways what visualisation is about — picture desired outcomes vividly so that they become reality. And in reality, people would in all probability find that next time they went walking, without thinking about it, they would choose the fifteen kilometre trip and not feel any worse for the experience.

Acquiring New Skills

For many years I have enjoyed recreational cycling. Until recently I had an older model mountain bike—one of the first models that came out. My limit was sixty kilometres a day with extreme exertion. There was one hill behind my home that I had tried on several occasions to ride up but found that I could not, and would always need to get off and walk to the top, a distance of perhaps half a kilometre. I planned on buying a new mountain bike—extra low gearing, an aluminium frame, a real performance model. For several weeks after I had ordered the model I wanted, I pictured myself riding everywhere. I pictured leaving the car at home in the garage and riding into town. I even pictured myself going where I had not been before on the old bike. But I would often picture myself riding up the hill just behind my home. I spent a lot of time on the new bike in my mind.

Just before I took possession of the new bike, I went for a last ride on the old one, starting off behind my home, and climbing the hill that I had never been able to climb before! It wasn't until I was at the top of the incline that I realised that I had done the impossible. On the old bike I had tried standing on the pedals as I used to as a teenager riding up hills. This still did not permit me to ride up that incline. But the pictures I had created of this event had done more than hundreds of hours and numerous attempts of riding had achieved before!

I saw myself riding up that hill on a bicycle. I saw it many times. I could do it—in my mind. I could then do the 'impossible' on the old bike!

The third area where visualisation can be of tremendous benefit is an area that I have practised, first without understanding how or why it worked, and then applying it to just about anything new that I take on. That is learning or developing new skills. Can you learn to weld simply by imagining the process? Yes, you can. That is how I learned this skill.

In Your New Image

I enrolled for a term at the technical college to learn arc welding. My first lesson was just as much a disaster as that of all the other students in my class. My pieces of steel fell apart, the welds were far from straight, and overall, the results were far from good.

At that time I was able to enjoy many long moments of mental absenteeism from my job. I was required to be there, at my desk physically, but no one said anything about being there mentally. So throughout the week I was welding. I would run the electrode over the steel plate and lay down a run of molten metal. I would do it again, and again in a different angle. I welded two pieces of metal together and cut them and welded them again. It was a very productive five days for me at work.

Although I had not touched the welding equipment for the week (I did not even own any welding equipment at that time), I was in the small welding booth when the tutor came in to see how I was progressing. He watched me for a few minutes then left, saying that he would help those who needed the instruction. He added that I didn't need his help that evening.

What was the difference? I had not touched the welding equipment for the week, had had only one session the week before at welding, and as I mentioned, the results were not good. Yet the difference was astounding, both to myself and to the tutor.

I believe most skills—carpentry, ceramics, jewellery, silversmithing, art metalwork, improving your score in a game of golf or tennis—can all be improved significantly through visualisation—the process of seeing yourself improve, of seeing yourself making things, of hitting the tennis ball, or swinging the golf club properly so your ball goes just where you want it to go.

I believe that, through visualisation, almost anything that is reasonable to expect is attainable. It is a matter of getting the right pictures, holding them and developing them.

Acquiring New Skills

These are examples of how you can improve your skills and performance merely by visualising the desired results.

RUNNING, JUMPING, CYCLING

You are already an athletic type or a sports person. With this technique, you are going to be shown something phenomenal — improving your performance merely by picturing yourself improving your output.

With this exercise, you need to see yourself performing at your present best, and then gradually increasing your output a little more each time. Let us look at running, although the same techniques apply to other sports — cycling, hurdles, marathon distance running, canoeing — in fact, anything where you will need a competitive edge over your rivals, where the rewards are there if you perform better than ever before.

Relax, picture yourself in pleasant surroundings as discussed before. Hold that picture of tranquility for a minute or two.

Picture yourself preparing for a race just as you have numerous times before. See yourself starting, and picture yourself running the whole race. Repeat this in your mind at least a couple of times. Get the feel of the day — the sun overhead, the sounds of the track, even the footsteps of the other runners near you. Ensure that the images you create of yourself in that race you are running in are as vivid and as realistic as you can get them.

Now run that race again in your mind. This time, see yourself for the first few seconds running that race as fast as you can. Now see yourself increase your speed slightly — your legs going even faster, and feel yourself edging slightly ahead of your competitors. Do not make the race seem ridiculous, all you want at this stage is a small increase in overall performance. See yourself maintaining that increased speed for the rest of the race. What does it feel like? Can you see the other athletes? Are they behind you? See yourself maintaining that speed and position until you reach the finishing line. How does it feel? What are you aware of—your surrounds, the people cheering you?

Run the same race in your mind several more times, or preferably over the next week or two, just with that increased performance that you were able to maintain in that last race.

Now it's time to give the race even more of your best. So get ready in your mind to run that race again.

Once the race has begun—you know what you are capable of, because for the last week or two you ran faster than you have ever run before. This time, you are going to see yourself running slightly faster than you did in those previous races—no superhuman forces are needed—merely creeping slightly and slowly ahead of your performance over the past couple of weeks.

See yourself maintaining that new lead over your competitors. What did that race feel like? What sounds are you aware of? Your images must be realistic. Maintain this new performance for a couple of weeks or more—remember, no superhuman endeavours are required, just a slight edge over your performance over the past couple of weeks in your imaginary races.

READING FASTER

Many years ago a friend was able to increase his reading speed from less than twelve pages an hour to somewhere around fifty or more pages an hour by visualisation alone, and gained the added benefit of increased comprehension and retention as well. Others have enjoyed this similar bonus.

Not only will your reading speed increase, but your enjoyment of reading, and the enjoyment of gaining increased knowledge from extra reading, will increase.

Relax, picture yourself in pleasant surroundings as discussed before. Hold that picture of tranquility for a minute or two.

Acquiring New Skills

Picture yourself preparing to read just as you have numerous times before.

What is the book you are holding? What colour is the cover? Is it a thick book? What does it look like, and feel like? Create the image of yourself reading and ensure that the picture is as vivid as you can get it.

See yourself reading the words of the book as you normally would read—slowly, perhaps word by word in your mind. Hold the book as you would if you were actually reading it.

Now increase the movement of your eyes over each line. Don't skim so fast that the process becomes ridiculous. All you want to achieve at this point is a slight increase in the speed at which your eyes flow over each line of the page. So see yourself reading each line slightly faster than you did before.

See yourself in your image maintaining that slightly increased speed. How does it feel?

See yourself reading at least several pages, always ensuring that you maintain that slightly increased speed, but never racing the process at all. See yourself turning the page, scanning the words as your eyes flow from line to line. You reach the bottom of the page, move your hands and turn the page.

See yourself maintaining that same speed for the next page, perhaps even the next chapter.

Repeat this reading process in your mind always—and I repeat always—ensuring that you are reading faster than the speed at which you used to read similar pages.

Now relax and imagine yourself reading a book—perhaps even the same book—at that same increased speed for a minute or two. This time, you are going to increase even that speed.

Picture yourself reading each line, your eyes going slightly faster over each word, over each line. Maintain this new speed. Again, no speed reading records should be attempted. All you want to achieve at this point is a slight increase in your reading ability over the speed you acquired during the previous weeks. See yourself reading each line of text, each line adds to a page, each page adds to a chapter — all at a speed faster than you have previously read. See yourself at every opportunity for the next two or three weeks maintaining this latest speed with greater comprehension.

Now see yourself enjoying reading more. You are reading faster, you are able to read more in the same time that you have available, you are appreciating reading far more than you ever did.

Whenever you read a book in between these exercises, make sure that you make every effort to maintain the speed you acquired during your exercises, As far as your mind is concerned, those exercises were for real, they weren't merely being done for entertainment. You may have to make a conscious effort to ensure your speed is maintained at first, but then it will become a newly acquired habit, and a good one.

Chapter 9 Work

For most people, work is one of the most important parts of their lives. They claim that work gives them self respect — it makes them feel they are someone in their society. It makes them feel they are pulling their weight within their group, that they are paying their taxes just like everyone else. Without that job, many people feel devastated. The loss of their job might well be their own fault, brought about through attitude, behaviour, incompetence, or — as has been occurring more and more frequently during the last decade — through downsizing of organisations and companies.

Yet how many people do you know who go to work each day knowing they will have a fantastically enriching eight hours? If you keep similar company to me, the answer will be not very many. We do our jobs, not because we like them, but because we have to. I cannot always see how that self respect component can come into it as one of the most important aspects of a person's working life!

Work is no longer secure. Work is no longer permanent. When I left school, I was asked to decide whether I wished to stay in my first job until I reached the age of sixty-five, or preferred early retirement at the age of sixty. It was expected of recruits in those days that most would stay on within the organisation until they reached retirement age. No more.

It is not always that jobs disappear. It is not always justified that we blame bad management that led to the downsizing.

Often categories of positions disappear. Other times, there is a demand for certain types of positions, at other times, there is no demand at all for those same positions.

DOWNSIZING AND RIGHT SIZING—THAT'S THE WAY THE COMMERCIAL WORLD IS GOING

Several years ago I was invited to work for an organisation—one of the largest organisations of its type in the Southern Hemisphere. The organisation had just cut its staff from nearly twelve hundred to a little over seven hundred in the weeks before I took up that position. Within months, that staff level had been cut to a little over five hundred.

About a year ago I was invited to attend a get-together of all previous staff. It was to say farewell, for the organisation had been cut to under one hundred to 'tidy things up' before being virtually abolished altogether. The party was held in the printing area, known locally as the factory. That area was large enough to hold everyone who attended that evening's celebrations, because there was no machinery left, no desks, no presses, and, of course, no people worked there.

This is one example only of the trends in employment these days as most large organisations carry out their 'downsizing' operations. Some refer to the process as 'right sizing'. Whatever it's called, the result is that jobs are no longer secure, careers are no longer secure, and the world ahead for most workers these days is often long periods of insecurity between short-term contracts.

The average person coming into the work force these days expects to change direction in their career at least three times, sometimes four. By changing direction, I don't mean correcting course by a degree or two to make sure they hit the target. I mean a full ninety degree turn into something quite new to them.

Work

A few years later, they will quite likely be faced with another full ninety degree turn. And then a decade on, yet another change in direction.

These changes will mean adjustments. They will mean retraining. They will mean moving to other cities. They will mean disruption from their security and their comfort to face the often unknown environment out there.

Some people adapt. Many don't.

SURVIVAL OF THOSE BEST SUITED TO THEIR ENVIRONMENTS

Yet there is not one aspect of all that is involved with changes in direction in career — reskilling, retraining, starting anew — that cannot be made easier with visualisation. Did you hear that? Let me repeat it. There is not one aspect of all that is involved with changes in direction in career that cannot be made easier with visualisation.

Between the ages of sixteen and about sixty-five, most people spend about one quarter of their total hours at work. With that investment in time, it should be worthwhile. It should be something we enjoy. It should be satisfying. It should be rewarding — and here I am not merely referring to the financial gains of the work.

Boredom can be one of the greatest stimulants known, if it is used constructively and, as I mentioned, as a stimulant. Boredom can drive us on to better things. We develop new skills, because we are bored with those that we now have. It can drive us further than all the gasoline in the car. It can take us further than we ever imagined. It will, if we use it to further develop what we already have.

Yet how many of us are prepared to wallow away our lives in total boredom? I would say that the answer would be quite a good portion of the work force today. We feel insecure. We cling to what we have, instead of trying something new. We don't want to rock the boat, because we don't know what lies ahead of us.

THERE'S A LONG, LONG HAUL YET

How many years do you have left in the work force? Maybe twenty? Maybe thirty? Isn't it worth the change? The courage you can develop through visualisation will give you the courage you need to move ahead. By moving ahead I don't mean just a small step. I mean a giant leap. The courage to overcome your handicaps and the obstacles that stand between you and where you want to go. Those obstacles, those psychological restraints — you lack the confidence to talk in public, the ability to communicate with others. This might be what is holding you back — or you think it does.

But ahead of each one of us, unless we prepare now for the future in the work force, is only further insecurity, going into the unknown. And without those survival skills, many will not survive emotionally and psychologically. By survival skills, I am not referring merely to education, although the right education, giving the right qualifications, will take you further in your working life than if you had no credentials at all. No, I refer to confidence, being able to take setbacks without each one becoming a devastating event. Changing direction with ease. Being able to adapt readily whenever and as often as is required for survival in the work force.

The workplace these days is very competitive. To keep pace with the changes, and with those attributes that employers want and need, one needs to do far more than merely move with the times. You need to ensure that you are at least one or two steps ahead of the others who will be competing for the same jobs. Dare I say it one more time? There is not one aspect of all that is involved with changes in direction in career that cannot be made easier with visualisation.

Work

Look around you. Do you have what it takes to move up the corporate ladder? Perhaps. Would new skills enhance your chance of moving up that ladder to further your career goals? Probably.

The dream of many people is to work for themselves. You do what you want to do, how you want to do it. You can be yourself. And working for yourself has rewards that no amount of paid employment will bring. It will bring a sense of satisfaction with it that most employees never experience. And herein lies another option in the workplace for those who are properly prepared for the future. They can work for themselves. Okay, I'll admit working for yourself is not always easy. You have to go out and get the contracts, the odd jobs, the work, if you are to survive. You will not be able to depend on a pay packet every fortnight. You may not be able to plan that holiday to the islands next year. But self employment, either through necessity or, as is often more preferable, through one's own choice, is a good alternative to queuing up for endless interviews. While you are writing numerous applications, attending interviews, you could be producing work that you enjoy.

Just look at some of the real benefits of working for yourself in your chosen field.

Self employment makes you feel liberated, not obligated to the masses. Your field of work assumes its rightful place amongst the other essential components of your life. You can be creative to the full limit of your capacity, and as creative as you like, with no restrictions placed on your creativity or talents. You can actually enjoy yourself, and feel really productive.

Self employment gives you a healthy level of self confidence. It's mentally stimulating, where you can use those talents, not relying on others to tell you what to do next.

You don't need to apologise to anyone for your output, or your actions. You really become what you are. You can attract work because you are enthusiastic about what you do. But this list really goes on and on—at least for the person in the right frame of mind, it does.

Remember that if others can do it, so can you.

THERE REALLY IS A BRIGHT FUTURE FOR YOU AMONGST THE CHAOS

But what is stopping you from being self employed right now? Whenever I ask people, they hesitate and fumble for the answer. Often it comes down to a lack of their own self confidence. They don't think they have what it takes to work for themselves. They don't know if they have the skills they would need. They are not sure that they would be able to make such a vast change overnight.

But that change need not be made overnight. It can be made over a year or more. That much-needed confidence can be developed over twelve months or more. Dare I say it one more time? There is not one aspect of all that is involved with changes in direction ...

Yes, let me reassure you that visualisation, used properly, will give you much of that confidence. I am not suggesting that your new business will run by itself merely by your lounging around, beer can in one hand, thinking about all the money that will roll in during the week. If you have this impression by now of visualisation, I suggest you stop reading right now, and start reading the book all over again! No, what visualisation will do for you is give you the confidence you will need to see yourself in your new business. If you lacked that confidence, and that in turn prevented you from making the move, then it will help. And the extent to which it will help you depends entirely on the amount of visualisation you do to develop that idea into a viable business.

Many small businesses all over the world have developed from an idea. The other necessity is need.

But look at some of the small businesses that have been developed from hobbies.

People have started successful small businesses from a hobby of welding — that hobby for at least one person became a viable business of making decorative wrought-iron gates. For another, a background as a hobby welder started the person in a business of making farm gates and other steel items that farmers needed but were often too busy to build themselves.

A keen gardener has more than once developed a successful cut flower market for florists, growing bulbs and flowers on a small acreage that the family owned.

Others have loved tropical aquariums, and have gone on from there to lease attractive aquariums to consulting firms and doctors who use the showpiece in their reception areas for the enjoyment and enrichment of their clients and patients.

Others have had a hobby of gardening, and have successfully gone on to develop this into a small business where they have grown tropical indoor plants and hired them to firms to add greenery and life to an otherwise desolate work environment.

Good cooks have gone on to specialise in providing pavlovas to businesses for their special occasions and birthdays for staff, or have gone into a catering service for those too busy or too ill-equipped to provide the service themselves.

IT'S YOUR IDEA. IT'S YOUR BUSINESS

The idea for a successful small business is limited primarily by lack of imagination. Once you have that spark to get you started, that good idea, then you have at least started on your journey forward. If you still cannot get an idea of what might interest you, scan the index of the Yellow Pages telephone directory. Every business imaginable is in there!

You are going to ask me, 'How on earth is visualisation going to help me start up my own business?' One does not need to be a psychic to predict questions such as that. In fact, I would be surprised if people did not ask it.

You have a hobby — welding, let us say. Visualise yourself developing your skills as a welder. I should point out that, apart from regulations that govern safety and insurance and other red tape that tries to limit self development, there is generally no requirement for a person operating such a business, anywhere, to be a fully qualified and certified operator. So if you have basic skills in whatever your hobby or interest, you can proceed from there. For some of the professions, there are basic requirements, such as a certain standard of education, the need to meet licensing requirements, the need to be registered with peer organisations that assess the standard of your training. But you can check out what is needed. But apart from these, which are few compared with the opportunities waiting for you, you will still have a wide choice of activities to consider.

But I haven't yet answered your question — how on earth is visualisation going to help you set up your own business?

You will need to visualise yourself providing the service of your business. It might be making charming wrought-iron gates for homes. It might be setting up and maintaining tropical fish tanks in reception areas. It might be providing cut flowers to the local market. Then see yourself providing that service to the people — your customers. See yourself carrying out the tasks in your business. See yourself cutting and welding the steel that will make the frame of the gate for the house down the road from you. Imagine yourself taking those cut flowers to the florists. See the pleasure on the florists' faces as you deliver them. See the flowers in the containers as you take them from the back of your vehicle and into the shop. See things as they could really be. See yourself as you would like to be in a year's time.

Live the life of the welder, making wrought-iron gates for the homes in your area. Weld in your mind during your lunchtime. Weld in your mind while you are on the bus going home from

Work

work, or on the way to work. See it all happening before your own eyes. Live the life you want to lead even before you begin working for yourself. And when the right time comes around ... what then?

SEE WHAT YOU WANT TO DO

That's easy. You have been making wrought-iron gates for the past twelve months. You have called on numerous clients, you have measured their driveways, you have cut and welded the steel. You have made those images of yourself in your own business so real that, now that the time has come for that change in your career, you are well equipped to handle the work.

And what of the stress and strain of facing the uncertainty?

Again, I did not have to be a psychic to predict that question either. There will be times of quiet, of quarrelsome customers, of bad weather that prevents you from working. But if you visualise all aspects of working for yourself, then you will be better equipped to handle the bad times, the bad moments, as well as the joys. Read that sentence again. And again. With visualisation, you will be better equipped to work for yourself, to be better off than you would otherwise have been.

In making changes of this magnitude, there is one problem you may face that visualisation will not be able to prepare you for — other people's negativism. Visualisation will not overcome this outside force that you will encounter. But the confidence you will have developed to carry on your business will help you. With your confidence, you should be able to merely pass off comments such as how badly you are going to fail, with a reply such as, 'I doubt it ... I have been doing it for so long now, that I don't think you know what you are talking about'. When the occasion arises, try it.

We've looked at work and the need for it in most people's lives. Now we will focus on some of the important aspects of the work habits that will move you further ahead.

MOVING AHEAD FOR ACHIEVEMENT

Progress in work, as in almost any endeavour in our lives, depends on our moving ahead, merely by definition. There are ways to achieve this, not by putting in longer hours, working on weekends, taking work home, but by visualising the desired outcomes associated with work. The protective achievements described now can be attained easily and painlessly, and, in my opinion, more efficiently than by just about any other method. The methods described here are based on past successes, and they are included here because they work, if properly applied.

In any work environment, much time is wasted by dithering around, the occupant of a desk suffering the time-wasting tasks of shuffling papers without being able to make a decision about what he or she should do next.

Much more time, in some work environments, is wasted merely by working inefficiently or by working slowly. While there may be good reasons for such attitudes, there is nevertheless scope for each individual to make progress. One should not always wait to be told how and what to do.

With visualisation, we can all plan for a more progressive day at work, one in which we achieve more, feel more fulfilled and provide a better service to our employers. That, surely, is one of the important functions of work, not merely to earn money, although this of course is important too.

One aspect of a job that can certainly be improved through visualisation is that of selling. Most businesses depend on this of their employees in one way or another. Even those providing a service, such as engineering consulting, or a design studio that provides computer-aided artwork for publications, can be seen as selling in one way or another. Any contact with the public, or users, in which there is face to face or verbal contact, can be considered as selling. Unfortunately many employees overlook the fact that without sales, without customers, their employer does not succeed, and with the decline in business profitability goes the employee's chances of even staying on.

Work

Good sales work begins in the minds of those selling the product or service. It is indeed an incredible salesperson who can just go and sell anything. These people do exist, they are rare, and they are to be admired. But for the rest of us, preparation is the key to successful selling.

By preparation in the mind, I am of course referring to rehearsing the whole process over and over again until the sales pitch, the hand movements, the showing of the product, the voice control and the body language, are exactly as you wish them to be for a successful sale.

In this regard, it is important to see not only the sales being made over and over again (and therein lie plenty of opportunities to make successful sales without losing a single client for the firm and at the same time build up considerable confidence) but to ensure that you have got the sales techniques just right.

Think for a moment about calling on a client cold. If you are unprepared, you will stumble over your words and will possibly be clumsy. But having rehearsed the skills required dozens — hundreds — of times beforehand, there is little chance of mistakes. Often there is little room for improvement, for you will have perfected your technique, gained confidence, worked out all the answers the client is likely to ask, and will see yourself closing the sale in the desired manner. And isn't that what successful selling is all about?

HOW TO ACHIEVE SUCCESS AT SELLING

A number of people I have worked with in this technique have achieved remarkable successes while on holidays, far from the clients they depend on for their own livelihoods.

How have they been successful? While they have been away from their familiar territory, they have been more relaxed, more receptive to ideas, and, most importantly, have found the time they never realised they had to practise in their minds all there

In Your New Image

is to know and do in their businesses. The results not only transformed their egos and their morale, but their income too!

To achieve successful selling, it is necessary to know the product. A good salesperson will visualise the product he is selling. That sounds frivolous, but it is surprising how many people trying to sell something of value are aware of only what they have read about it in technical literature, and have memorised this. The result is that they can recite the information about it, but they do not know the product intimately. They don't know how it feels. They are not aware of how heavy it is, or how big it is, or what it is really like to hold, and turn over. If you want to part with something, it is necessary to really become familiar with those goods first.

And the same applies to services. We might be selling surveying, or land subdivision for a new real estate development. Look beyond the piece of paper on which the plans will be drawn. See the development in your mind. Picture the houses there, on each of the blocks. See the people there, what they look like. What type of people are they in this exclusive development? It is surprising the difference picturing the right people in the subdivision can make to the person's success in selling the real estate to the right people for the right price!

Again, people I have worked with in this technique have reported that visualising the whole concept of the development has made a big difference to their results. Some reported they had not even put people into the blocks before. But how did they become successful? They saw the whole picture of what the subdivision would be like. They felt it, smelled the fresh clean air. They saw the big houses, and the families, and watched the children enjoying themselves in the playground. Then their enthusiasm was easily passed on to the clients who bought this model subdivision from someone who believed in what they were selling. It became something the clients really wanted.

Work

Sales people are not the only ones in work who have to sell. Often employees have to present data to the firm's directors. They have to instil confidence in their peers that they have done a good job, perhaps as a sales manager who directs staff, or trains them to succeed.

Presentations have become an important tool in boardroom meetings. The staff member who fumbles and stammers over every little point he or she is trying to get across to their peers is only going to make one impression, and that will not be a favourable one! Yet month after month, week after week, perhaps for years unless they are replaced, the same people go on making the same mistakes and fail to impart their knowledge or impress those who matter.

Few realise that such techniques are rather easily overcome with proper preparation. One does not need to be the most receptive reader to know by now that this is achieved through visualisation. Visualisation in preparing for a presentation, as in just about any undertaking, can be the most effective, simplest and longest lasting tool there is, if applied adequately and persistently enough. And unlike those poor souls who make the same wimpy presentation for years without improving, with visualisation, the results can be remarkable after only a relatively short time

One man I worked with had to give a speech. He was inaudible, his was jittery, his voice soft — almost inaudible — and the impact he made was close to nothing. Several weeks later he was required to give another speech. This time, there was a genuine applause, with congratulations coming from all directions of the room. The difference? He hadn't spoken to any group between the two speeches, he hadn't gone to elocution lessons. Because he realised his previous performance was so bad, he agreed to visualise himself standing in front of forty people — all his peers — and giving the most dynamic presentation he could deliver. He saw his audience. He knew them personally. He knew the room. But since the first dismal occasion, he had visualised himself in that room with his peers. He saw them looking back at him, eager to hear what he had to tell them. For some weeks he saw himself out in the front of the podium, with his brief notes he glanced at only occasionally, talking in a loud, confident tone. He felt the atmosphere of the room, he saw everything as it really was. And when it was time to present his talk to the group of colleagues, he had forgotten the nervousness he had experienced only weeks earlier.

LEARN TO TALK TO PEOPLE

A friend of mine a little time ago had to travel interstate to attend the launching of his book. As he was not a public speaker by any means, this thought made him rather nervous. His publisher had asked him to talk for about five or ten minutes about the book. The occasion of the launch was an annual conference of an important organisation associated with the topic of the book.

He was lucky. He was given about four weeks notice. I suggested to him that he prepare notes that he could refer to, but to visualise the outcome. Together we worked through just what he could expect to encounter. He was able to picture the large room with displays around the walls, and products that were to be demonstrated. He could see about two hundred people there, all eager to hear what he would tell them about the subject of his book. He saw in his mind the artificial lighting (the launch was to take place in the evening). He felt the mood of the room.

On launch day, he was quite different to what I had expected him to be. Although the evening did not go exactly as he had planned, through rescheduling of events at the last moment, he nevertheless gave a superb presentation. The result was the audience seeing someone with confidence who really knew his subject. Many there that evening bought his book. He had not underestimated the power of visualisation to overcome what he had seen previously as his shortcomings.

With events such as talking in public (such as my friend's book launch, or in selling), it may be unwise to lose all nervousness. A residual amount might be an asset to drive the energy you need. You do not want a presentation or a sales pitch to be flat and without emotion.

IT'S A GIVE-AND-TAKE WORLD

Sensible employees see work as a two-way process between themselves and their employers. They want to receive good working conditions, good pay, respect and loyalty. In return, they would like to feel they give the employer good value for his money. With all the good intentions in the world, this is not always achieved.

There are procrastinators, and there are those who fail to work efficiently. There is seldom a valid reason why efficiency cannot be improved with visualisation. We know what it takes to work well. We know our job well enough. We know all there is to be done at work. Yet, for many, efficiency might be as low as fifty to sixty percent of maximum capacity. Why? We do not do things right. We take far too long on a simple task. We take too long planning the irrelevancies and the trivia that do not matter to the job, to the employer and especially to the employee. Yet we still work inefficiently.

Image the results and your daily output if you were to be paid for your efficiency. Wouldn't you work smarter and harder? Of course you would. You would very quickly learn what you could do in half the time. You would stop procrastinating. You would spend part of your day, indeed, I am sure you would possibly spend much of your leisure time as well, working out ways to ensure you were no longer inefficient and get the job done in half the time.

So imagine you are being paid for doubling your output. This would indeed be a marvellous and encouraging thought for many, but try to appreciate how much benefit the employer is going to receive, how much more loyalty you will earn, if you could work this efficiently.

Seeing yourself working like this is easy. And once you have visualised the whole process of working at this level of efficiency for a few weeks, put it into practice in your real job. You will probably find that your work does improve in quality during that time, merely because there is never a cut-in point at which time the effectiveness suddenly starts. As you visualise the desired outcomes in your work (or in just about any other endeavour), you will notice that the desired improvements and changes are introduced in a most subtle and innocuous way, slowly but becoming increasingly effective the more you visualise the desired results.

Let us now consider how to visualise correctly what is needed for the points covered so far in this chapter.

INCREASING ABILITY AND EFFICIENCY AT WORK

Take a deep breath and let it out slowly and relax, and count to ten. Picture yourself in a peaceful setting for a minute or two, such as on a beach or in a meadow.

Imagine yourself at your work with numerous tasks to do. You are usually so busy there that you do not have time to become organised to plan your day so that you work efficiently to achieve a high output. See yourself as you would be on a normal day. Watch yourself at work in your mind for at least a few minutes or more.

See yourself through another's eyes performing your work — lots of it, but with no coordination or apparent system to your day — your typical working day.

Now picture yourself sitting at your desk or place of work, taking stock of all the work you have, mentally categorising the

Work

tasks so that work of a similar nature is grouped together. You can picture as many groups of work as you like.

Look at the whole day's work (or other convenient period of work that might be appropriate to your workplace). How many groups are there? Is all the work now appropriately grouped according to the nature of the tasks? See these groups clearly.

See yourself at your place of work through another's eyes, looking at the groupings, and checking that they are correct. How do you see yourself?

Now picture yourself taking the largest and the most difficult group of work, pulling it towards you (the tasks you are picturing could well be symbolic of the real work) so that you have only one lot of work there.

See yourself through another's eyes, sitting there with the group of work, looking at it, feeling pleased with yourself that you are going to get through this so you can move on to one of the other groups of tasks.

Picture yourself working through that group—the largest and the most difficult, without interruption or disturbance until you have finished all the duties you are required to perform. Watch the number diminish (you can represent the actual number by some figure).

Now see yourself writing a large sign on a piece of paper 'finished', and move the group to one side.

See yourself through another's eyes looking at the groupings you have yet to complete. Watch this person—you—decide to take the next group, the next most difficult group of work, and pull it towards yourself. Notice your face. Are you confident? Pleased?

Now see yourself taking the first piece of work from that next group—these pieces of work are different from those that comprised the first group—and tackle the first task there. Picture yourself working your way through each task in this category until they are all gone. Again, see yourself write out another sign that reads 'finished' and put that on the completed pile of work.

Think of how pleased you feel at achieving this, in such an orderly manner. Push these imaginary tasks, still in a group, beside the first finished group.

Repeat this process until you have worked your way through all the groups of tasks and have added a 'finished' sign on each of them.

Mentally arranging your workload soon translates to action at the place of your employment, and is very effective in getting people thinking in terms of efficiency and far greater output. Seeing yourself performing better and more efficiently soon makes you behave according to the way you have seen yourself working, developing this attitude as a new habit. Within a short time your output should have at least doubled, and orderliness increased by an even greater amount.

STOP PROCRASTINATING

Take a deep breath and let it out slowly and relax, and count to ten. Picture yourself in a peaceful setting for a minute or two, such as a beach or a meadow.

Imagine yourself at your normal place of work, faced with a lot of work that you have been putting off. See it clearly, identify each component of the tasks facing you. It is important to visualise this scene as clearly and as vividly as if you were at your work.

See yourself through another's eyes, sitting at your desk (or place of work) and looking at it. What is the scene like? Does the outstanding work comprise mainly paperwork, accounts that have been left unpaid, letters that need responding to?

Now see yourself looking at the pile of work, and reaching out to take the first piece of work from the top. And notice that, as you remove the first piece of work, the pile remaining shrinks slightly.

Work

Picture yourself doing the work required of you to complete this task efficiently and properly and to the satisfaction of your supervisor.

Imagine yourself working right through the task, to completion, and putting the work onto another heap beside you.

Now picture yourself looking at the remaining pile of work and reach out and take the next item from that pile. Watch that pile as you remove the work, see how that pile shrinks even more.

Watch as you complete the next task.

Looking at yourself at your desk or place of work through another's eyes, watch yourself working at this latest task, seeing how you work at it efficiently and swiftly. Notice what you do to speed up the process so that you do not spend any unnecessary time on it.

Look at yourself at your desk, completing the latest task, and putting it with the first piece of work you pictured yourself finishing.

Now look at that pile of outstanding work, and reach out to take the next item. You realise that this is a piece that you do not find interesting at all — possibly the main reason why you have put off completing it for so long. But, in the picture you are creating, see yourself take the work, look at it and immediately begin doing whatever is necessary to complete this task.

How does it feel to have finished something you have been putting off for so long? Do you feel a sense of elation? Of satisfaction? Of relief? Possibly you feel all these emotions.

Watch as you complete the task, and add that to the pile of completed work. Watch this pile grow as you add the latest achievement to the top.

See yourself taking the next piece of work — even more unpleasant — boring, difficult perhaps — and putting it in front of you at your desk or workplace to tackle it. And as you

In Your New Image

remove this latest piece of work, take note of how the original pile of outstanding work had diminished considerably.

You can speed up the process in your mental images. But in reality, I would be surprised if you did not achieve more than three times the output that you have been used to. This method alone is the only way I know of getting through work that is not stimulating enough to warrant doing straight away but is nevertheless essential for you to do for the sake of your employer and your job.

Simply by speeding up the process and seeing yourself completing each task, and not delaying taking on the next, and the next, your work will soon be finished.

PREPARING FOR A JOB INTERVIEW

Take a deep breath, let it out slowly and relax, counting to ten. Picture that peaceful setting.

Picture yourself getting ready for the interview, deciding what clothes you will wear. See yourself setting out on your bed your best dress and jacket or shirt. Now see yourself in front of the mirror making those final adjustments, knowing that you are going to look your best as you attend that important interview.

See yourself still very relaxed and confident, opening the front door of your home, your briefcase or satchel in your other hand, closing the door after you. Next, picture yourself getting into the car and driving out of your driveway. Make sure at this stage you still feel relaxed and at ease, unruffled by the pending interview.

Picture yourself outside the premises where you will be interviewed. Look around you. Notice the building, the windows, how many floors there are, take note of the entrance. Make this image as clear and as detailed as you possibly can.

Look at yourself getting into the elevator and pressing the button for the floor you were asked to report to, or reporting to

Work

the reception desk, giving the receptionist your name, your purpose in being there, and whom you wished to see.

It is important to see yourself walking confidently, slowly but deliberately, remembering that you are the person they want to employ. See yourself regarding this interview merely as a formality, an occasion where you will remain full of self confidence.

Picture yourself being introduced to the interviewers — say there are three people whom you will be talking to.

See in your mind one of them asking you to sit down. In your picturing, do not let yourself rush any event — just take your time and act as if you already have the position you have applied for. Feel happy in yourself, pleased to be in this situation. This is important, as the way you feel at this stage will determine how you come across to the interviewers. So see yourself sitting, relaxed, in front of the other three. What are they wearing? Are they wearing suits? Are the women wearing long dresses? And what colour are their scarves or jackets? See every detail, as though you really are there talking to these people about your future.

Feel what it is like as you listen intently to their questions, then respond with your considered reply. Hear yourself speak confidently in a full, clear voice — indicating that you are knowledgeable in the subject, and capable. See yourself — hear yourself give another answer to one of their questions. And see and hear yourself reply to more questions.

Hear yourself in your mind asking the interviewers about the firm — information you were not able to ascertain about the company before your interview. Hear yourself ask how your position will fit into the structure of the firm. Hear their reply.

Realise that you have been there for almost one hour, actually enjoying yourself talking to the staff of the new firm you will soon be working for. What does this moment of the interview feel like? See yourself still sitting in that chair in front of the interviewers, relaxed but certainly not slouching.

In Your New Image

The interview is nearing its end. Imagine yourself standing up, shaking hands with the people you have enjoyed talking to, giving them a warm smile as you depart.

Now see yourself leaving that interview room, walking away from the door, confidently and proudly, as if you have just been told that you have been appointed to the position you so much wanted. Feel that moment. See that occasion — you have been appointed to the position you wanted. What does it feel like? Experience it in every detail — the emotion of realising that you were successful in securing that difficult position, feeling the joy of knowing you will be starting in that firm in the next few weeks, maybe even sooner.

See yourself go home, relax in the glory and the knowledge that you have been appointed to the position. Don't stop visualising that — that you have already been appointed to the position. If you feel that way, believe it, know that it's as good as true, then your mind will let you, on the real occasion, act as though it is true.

Your confidence will come across and show you as a successful, competent person.

Rehearse these scenes in your mind from the moment you are asked to attend an interview for the position. If you feel confident that you will be asked in for an interview, begin imagining the scenes just like these as soon as you post off your application.

In this scenario, it is essential to see yourself as calm, see yourself sitting comfortably before three people, and talking confidently with those people. It is also essential to picture yourself as being the successful candidate. Remember, your subconscious mind will not let you down on the day.

STARTING A NEW JOB

Take a deep breath and let it out slowly and relax, and count to ten. See yourself in a tranquil setting.

Work

Picture yourself getting ready for your first day in your new job. Picture yourself getting dressed, tidying yourself up and brushing your hair. Look in the mirror. What do you see? You will notice yourself—the real you—calm, confident, eager to start an exciting new day. Feel good about yourself as you look at yourself in the mirror.

See yourself through someone else's eyes, as you calmly go about your preparation in readiness for leaving your home to travel to the new job.

Now see yourself closing the door. What is the weather like outside? Is it sunny? Are there leaves on the trees? Is there a gentle breeze blowing that early in the morning? Move the tips of the small branches in your picture. Yes, you realise, there is a light breeze blowing that morning. Feel the air. Is it crisp? Fresh? Is it warm? Make it as you wish, but make it real.

Calmly and with confidence, and full of spirit and excitement, you stroll down the road to your transport, or to your garage to get into your car. Hear the door close. Feel the car as you mentally start the motor.

See yourself going along the road either in the public transport or driving your car. You feel good, and relaxed and comfortable with yourself.

Now see yourself approaching the new building where you will be working from this day on. What is its construction material? Is it block? Or is it brick? Is it constructed from some other building material? Describe it—remember, you were there just recently for your interview.

Picture that doorway. Stand back for a minute or two, feeling calm and relaxed, as you watch several people walk through that door. What are they wearing? Make them seem real people in your mental picture.

See that door open and feel yourself, see yourself, walk through the door and to the elevator.

See yourself through another's eyes as a calm and relaxed person full of confidence, eager to start your new life right there.

In Your New Image

See that person who is you look up as the elevator doors open. Are there other people getting out, or in? Picture yourself joining them as they get in the elevator with you.

Imagine that you have arrived at your floor, and your new supervisor is there to greet you. You shake hands warmly, smile a genuine greeting. Picture yourself in that room you were shown the other day during your interview, looking around. You know this area well. You had pleasant feelings about it last time you were here. You still have those pleasant feelings now.

See yourself through another's eyes being introduced to the new colleagues you will be working with. There's your desk or machine over by the window, or the far wall. Then look at it, feeling relaxed and happy to be there.

Now look at yourself at your machine or at your desk as through another's eyes for a full minute. You look so relaxed and comfortable. You belong there. You feel good about being there. What is the view like from your window? Can you look out across the town? Over a park? What can you see through the window? Look outside for a moment and try to notice all the objects there.

Now picture yourself at that desk or the machine, beginning to work. You know what you are doing. Look at everything on that desk, the paper, the manuals, the computer and the work that you will begin doing shortly. Or if a machine, notice what colour it is, the paint work, its condition. How big is it?

This scene must, like all the others, be clear, vivid, and you must feel relaxed and very, very comfortable.

Hold that scene of yourself there for at least another two minutes, still feeling good about the day.

Now see someone approach you and ask if you would like to join the others for morning tea. How does it feel to be asked? Are you smiling? Are you looking forward to light conversation with your work mates? Are you still relaxed?

How many other people are there with you during your break? Are they standing, or sitting at a table? What sort of table

Work

is it? Picture it as you would expect to find it. That room must seem real to you.

Through another's eyes, see the afternoon light dim as you prepare to go home. You say goodbye to your colleagues and leave your work area. You have felt good about this day in your images.

Rehearse these scenes every opportunity you get from when your hear that you have been given the new position to when you begin, particularly on the couple of days and evenings before starting. Because on that first day, if you have relived these scenes enough, it won't seem strange, because you have lived it many, many times before. Your mind will believe that you have already worked there for at least a week, maybe a fortnight, and by then you will have settled into the routine comfortably anyway. This just shortens that process considerably.

GIVING BUSINESS PRESENTATIONS

Take a deep breath and let it out slowly and relax, and count to ten. Picture yourself in a very peaceful setting.

Picture yourself getting ready for the presentation you have been asked to give at your work. See in your mind the overhead transparencies on your desk in front of you. Don't pick them up, just notice them. They do not worry you, because you feel so calm and relaxed. Those overhead transparencies represent your work, your knowledge. You feel good about yourself when you see them.

Now pick them up one at a time, slowly, holding them up to the light. Feel calm in yourself as you handle each one. There are a number of them, and you check each one individually. Take your time. Handle them slowly, and do not rush this process. You have a lot of time ahead of you.

Through another's eyes, see yourself put them neatly into a folder. Check that your limbs and neck are indeed relaxed.

In Your New Image

Relax them some more if you can. Now see yourself close that folder and stand up. You still feel good, because you feel relaxed.

Picture yourself walking into the room where you will make your presentation.

What can you see as you mentally stand at the doorway and look in? Is there a large wooden table in the big room? Is the overhead projector there near the front of the room? How many chairs are there? How are they arranged? Are they around the table, and against the walls?

Are the blinds over the windows open or closed as you look in the doorway? Are the lights on? How bright is the room?

Now pay particular attention to how relaxed you feel. This is important.

You feel good about going into the room because you know you have prepared yourself well for this presentation. It is important to you, and to your firm. That is why they have asked you to give it.

Now see yourself in your mind walk slowly, confidently and calmly to the front of the room where you will stand and talk. Are you still relaxed? Make sure that as you picture this scene, your limbs, neck and back muscles are very relaxed. There should be no tension in your muscles at all, and you should be experiencing no mental tension.

Through another's eyes, look at yourself standing in the front of the room. There are only a couple of other people there, as you arrived early to prepare the room for the presentation. You have not a care in the world. You are very relaxed and you feel so comfortable.

Now see the room through your own eyes. You notice a person arrive, acknowledge your presence and take a seat. Look at that person, but feel at ease in their presence.

In your image, allow a couple more people to enter the room. They sit down.

Work

Your supervisor arrives and comes up to you to check on something. You are happy to see him or her, and feel comfortable that they have taken an interest in your pending moment. Now watch your supervisor take a seat in the room.

Still being conscious that you are physically and mentally relaxed, you watch more people come into the room, not surging in, but coming in slowly. You have a lot of time, so allow them to come in one at a time, look around them, and sit down.

Feeling relaxed, you see the number increase to the size of the audience you expected. They are all there.

Stand there, in your image, in front of them, for at least two, preferably four or five minutes, just looking at them. Look around the room. Look into each of the faces, into their eyes. See them as people. See them as individuals. Look at each one carefully.

You feel relaxed. You feel proud. You know you look good up there. You feel confident. You are the picture of the perfect presenter.

Now picture yourself beginning. Hear yourself talking in a strong, loud voice so that the people at the back of the room can hear clearly.

Hold that picture of yourself talking for several minutes. See yourself breaking up your talk as you put the transparencies on the overhead projector. See them shining on the screen behind you, one after the other. Look at them in your image, their colour, the blocks, the lines and diagrams. See yourself pointing to features on them, talking about what each part represents or means.

Now look up from the projector and notice the audience listening intently as you tell them what they have come to hear from you.

Through another's eyes, see yourself going through the transparencies. See yourself from another's perspective, out in front of the audience, showing transparency after transparency.

In Your New Image

Make sure you are relaxed. After all, this is an image in your mind. There is nothing to be afraid about.

See yourself making several small mistakes in what you say. But feel yourself correcting those mistakes without letting them upset you at all. It is small mistakes that will make you human to others. Carry on talking, feeling good, and calm, and enjoying this experience.

If you have been given more than a few days to prepare for the presentation, you can practise it and practise it over and over again in your mind. On the actual day, you will have given your presentation so many times that the real one will seem no different from those you have rehearsed.

WORKING FOR YOURSELF

Take a deep breath and let it out slowly. Relax and count to ten. Picture yourself in a peaceful setting for a minute or two.

For this scenario, you will already have decided on what type of business you want to go into for yourself. It can be anything you choose — small manufacturing, retail, or service. The idea is to see yourself not only performing your new line of work, but feeling comfortable in the fact that you have broken ties with your past working environment, and have taken the challenge of facing the world on your own. You need to overcome that fear of the unknown, and with visualisation, you can do it.

Picture yourself in front of the business you have always wanted to undertake. Picture your premises where you will be working. Feel the atmosphere of the premises — is it light or dark? Are the lights on? Are the premises big or small? Get a clear mental image of your proposed premises. In your mind, continue picturing this area for at least a few minutes.

See yourself working at your chosen activity. Pick up the merchandise, or a tool, and use it. Turn it over.

Work

Now see yourself applying the tools or tidying the stock on the shelves. Make this scene as realistic as you possibly can. Add the colour, make sure it is exactly as you would like it to be.

From another's eyes, watch yourself going about your business in your new premises. Watch this person who is you going through the work that is typical of the business. You will watch yourself being composed and fitting in well in this environment.

Think for a few minutes about the work you have left behind to come to this business, and feel good inside about your move and about your decision to change your circumstances.

Through your own eyes, see yourself performing the tasks typical of the business again. What are you doing? Do these tasks for several minutes, or for as long as you are able to hold the image of your proposed activity in your mind.

Alternate the scenes you are observing between those through another's eyes, and as you would see them yourself. Watch yourself comfortably at work in your premises.

The idea in this imagery is to watch yourself repeatedly at work in your own business, enjoying yourself and feeling confident.

Watch scenes of yourself working or providing a service to your clients as often as you can. You should extend this period well beyond the minimum three-week period that I have suggested elsewhere. It is likely that such a big decision will not have been taken lightly, so you will possibly have had a long time to plan the type of business you have wanted, and put a lot of activities into place already. If you can use the time between first making that decision and actually beginning the task of accepting the reality of the move without all those doubts that most people experience with such a move you will be well rewarded.

Chapter 10 Making Friends

Loneliness can be one of the worst curses of any society. It is very widespread, and is becoming more so, in advanced countries. It reflects our belief that society has not and will not accept us. We lack the ability to make friends, because we are shy. We fear rejection, so we are happier (slightly, at least) by not putting ourselves forward to other people who might turn us down. We don't ask a person of the opposite sex for a date because we are shy, and anyway, he or she might turn us down, and that would be more devastating than going up to them, talking pleasantly to them and asking them out to dinner.

The results can be eternal loneliness.

We might meet an interesting stranger who would at first appear to have a lot in common with us—if only we could communicate with them and tell that person exactly what our interests are. We lose the chance to develop possibly a long and lasting friendship, because we do not have the courage, or as some would say, the nerve, to say, 'hey, want a cup of coffee? I'd like to hear more about this'. The result? Loneliness, and a missed opportunity (again) to develop possibly an interesting and long friendship.

In life's tortuous deviance, we are the ones who miss out—the people who want friendship and companionship more than anyone else.

Yet it is surprising how little effort it takes to turn around this situation. After using the right visualisation techniques and the

Making Friends

right images you will go boldly forward and change your loneliness into terrific and meaningful friendships. And it is important to realise that quite often the person we would like to talk to is feeling exactly the same, craving friendship and companionship. Perhaps they are, just like you, waiting for someone to get the courage and talk to them.

I admit that many people are reluctant to begin conversations with people they do not know, or have not been introduced to, because they are afraid of what the other person might be like. While there are people in any society whom we can genuinely claim we are better off not having as our friends, I believe that such claims are greatly exaggerated. Yes, we do meet undesirable people we would like to run away from. But in any community, the percentage of such people is very small. The chance of meeting even one of them is very small indeed.

One other reason we might be reluctant to start a conversation or friendship is that we feel deep inside us that the friendship won't last, and therefore we will be saddened by the loss of yet another friend. People do move on. People do move interstate, or overseas. Much of the population of the world these days is highly mobile, brought about by affluence and the transport systems that provide low cost travel. Yes, we will lose friends. Yes, some friendships will be short.

But on the other hand, many friendships can nevertheless enrich our lives for as long as they last, however short or long that period might be.

But once we have developed our own self confidence, built up our self esteem, then we are far better equipped to deal with the loss of a friend. Is it better to have a new friend for a short time, or have no friend at all? I believe the first option is more rewarding for what it can offer us rather than the hollow that an empty life will bring us.

WINNING IN THE LOTTERY OF LIFE

But it is not only in friendships that we face the hollowness of loneliness. It is in relationships that might not last. It is in marriages that might not last. But is it better to take a chance, meet someone who could provide us with all the happiness and security that we could ask for, than not risk anything, except an empty life? Such arguments are a little like buying a lottery ticket. Is it better to buy a ticket and have a small chance of winning a substantial prize than not buying that ticket, saving the two dollars, and never winning a thing in our lives?

The game of life in relationships is like a lottery, except that the odds of winning in this lottery are far, far higher than they are with a monetary lottery. Okay, the cost is higher, but the rewards can be more substantial too.

So if a shy person wants to overcome this handicap, launch out, meet more people, perhaps that person sitting alone, is it expecting the impossible for that chance event to succeed?

I don't think the risk of rejection need be seen as very high at all. If the potential rewards are there, as in a deep and lasting relationship, what has the person got to lose by saying yes? And if you do not talk to the person, what is lost then? If the person should turn you down, that is the same as not asking them at all. But if the response is affirmative, then it has all been worthwhile. And in this short chapter, we will take you through the imaging necessary to conquer that fear and nervousness of talking to other people, especially members of the opposite sex.

The correct visualisation will give you the confidence and, really, the ability to talk to other people that you would dearly like to meet. It is the means of gaining that air of assurance, of feeling good about what you are doing, that will make the difference. In this scenario, try a range of settings that might be appropriate to you.

Here's how you can make decent friends and lasting relationships.

MAKING FRIENDS

Take a deep breath and let it out slowly. Relax and count to ten.

Picture yourself at your magical spot in your world where you feel safe and secure, and comfortable because of its inherent beauty and feel.

Imagine yourself in a line at the checkout. The line is moving slowly, ever so slowly, and you know you and all the people after you will be there for a long, long time.

In your mental picture, put someone there that you would like to talk to. Make that person of similar age, but they could be of either sex.

In your mind, you are aware of their presence, but you do not fear any contact with anyone because all the customers are intent on getting through the checkout and on their way home.

While you are still relaxed and feeling calm, picture yourself turning around to that person you have created. Now see yourself take a deep breath and speak slowly, confidently and in a loud voice. It does not have to be an intellectual or stimulating bit of conversation—just enough to get the words flowing.

Now, through another's eyes, watch as the other person turns to you, nods, smiles and replies to you.

Watch as this person then makes another remark to you. You feel good in your mind because at least you have started the words flowing from both parties.

Now see yourself replying to this person again. Watch as this person in your mind replies to your comment.

In your mind's picture you have time to consider at length what you are going to say to the other person.

Think carefully about the next sentence you are going to say, then in your mind's picture, see yourself saying it to this person. Watch their reply.

Now, through another's eyes, see the scene of the two of you talking—not a great, philosophical debate, but rather just idle talk to pass the time while you all wait to be served.

In Your New Image

Watch the others in the shop, and notice that they are not talking to one another — it's only you two and perhaps one or two much further back who are engaged in any form of conversation.

Watch this scene of the two of you engaged in conversation, both apparently enjoying these moments.

See yourself move along the queue slightly, and speak to the other person again and again. Remember, you can take your time to think up what to say, and you should see yourself as well composed, relaxed and confident while you all wait out your time in that long queue.

Through another's eyes, watch the scene from further over in the shop, and see the two of you both smiling as you communicate, and apparently pleased that you both have someone interesting to talk to while the queue moves slowly forward.

Now you are only a couple of minutes from the checkout counter. In your mind's picture, see yourself turn to the other person, and say, again, confidently and in a slow, clear voice, 'hey, why don't you let me buy you a cup of coffee?'

This might seem oversimplified, but it isn't. You will be surprised at just how many people are waiting to meet other people, form new friendships, meet someone they can enjoy a cup of coffee with, and a friend they can call a companion.

All it takes is that brief moment of starting the conversation, and, even if you get no response at first, do not give up. Don't forget, they could have been just like you — shy, reserved, and feeling uneasy the first time someone spoke to them. It might not have happened in their lives any more than similar incidents have happened in yours. So, in your mental pictures of yourself starting a conversation, build into the pictures some reluctance on the part of the stranger, until you have exchanged at least a few sentences. But, in real life, realise the point at which such an attempt might be fruitless. There are some people who simply do not want to communicate. But many people will, given the

Making Friends

chance from you, relish the opportunity to talk to someone else ... and enjoy that cup of coffee!

Chapter 11 Feeling Good

What is the difference between having an ordinary day, and feeling good? This is possibly one of the harder things in life to define. Possibly it is that everything seems to go right for us. We can have a lot of control over that part of our lives. And perhaps too it is not caring about the little things in life, those insignificant, trivial things that want to weigh us down unless we banish them forever.

I would have to be the first to agree with you when I hear you say that we have to worry about things — how else are we going to see our lives in perspective if we don't? There is a big difference between those things in our lives that we need to be concerned with, and those everyday events that, on their own, don't seem to contribute much to our wellbeing.

Let me give you some examples of the difference. Say your daughter is expecting her child, and she has been experiencing complications. You know that her husband or partner is very concerned about her and the safety of their yet unborn child. Only a foolish, cold-hearted parent would not be concerned with such an event. It is natural to be concerned, to worry, about those immediate to us — our loved ones.

DECIDE WHAT IS WORTH WORRYING ABOUT ... AND DISMISS THE REST

You might have received some bad news — most of us do from time to time. It might be a diagnosis, yet unconfirmed — about a serious illness that our doctor suspects that we have, but won't commit an opinion until his tests reveal otherwise, or confirm his beliefs. That worry too is natural. There are indeed hundreds of events we could cram into a single day that we should be genuinely concerned about. One does not need a good imagination to list even a small number of these.

But the ones that we have control over are those events that we let bother us. These, in isolation, are more nuisance value and get in the way of our getting on with real living and hold us back. Quite often we put things off until we feel better about ... well, whatever it is that is bothering us.

Need such events really bother us? We might be upset about a remark that our boss made, perhaps even in fun. We take it seriously. Should we take that remark seriously? Perhaps not. If this happened to you and you are concerned over the implications of this remark, that's fine, wonder about it, ascertain from your boss what is wrong, and act on your findings. Or better still, dismiss that remark as being of no real significance and get on with your life. However, be warned that too much of this indifference can upset some bosses even more, so you will need to decide where you draw that line between concern and indifference. You boss might be the type of person who speaks his mind without realising what is on it. Yes, by all means be concerned if such incidents are justified, if not, then you get the message. Life is more important than worrying about such remarks.

You might be concerned that you have received a letter saying that your mortgage repayment is overdue. You might have made that payment just recently — admittedly a few days late — and the bank is getting upset that your payment has not yet been credited to your account.

Again, a sensible person will react in one of two ways — hopefully as appropriate according to the real circumstances.

If that payment was made, but late, and you know that by now the bank will have been satisfied with your money, dismiss the whole affair and get on with whatever it is that is more important than dwelling over your forgetfulness and the bank's delayed response in crediting your statement.

If, however, you have not made that payment, you cannot make that payment because you have no money, well, then that's different. There are some options, depending on your circumstances, whether you are a regular defaulter, or just slack about making payments on time. Such real situations can be fixed relatively easily — get the bank to take the money out of your account each fortnight instead of going to the bank and occasionally forgetting about it and receiving their nasty letters. If you genuinely cannot make the payment this week, let the bank know about your circumstances. Despite all we hear about the coldness of many lending institutions, they are generally more lenient and warm-hearted if we tell them the circumstances and work out a plan with them so they can see that they will receive their money in time. But whatever you do, the message I am telling you is — if you don't need to worry, then don't. If you do, then put something into place, get your day moving again, and get on with your life.

TRY FEELING GOOD ABOUT YOURSELF

It is surprising how much a lot of people let small things rule their lives.

But wouldn't the ideal world be one in which we didn't have a care in the world? Indeed it would. Try to make your world such a place.

When we feel good about ourselves, generally the rest of the world sings along with us. Unless, of course, there are circumstances beyond our control and beyond our reach that we can do little to put right. But generally, if we are happy, then the rest of those little things that weigh us down seem to disappear.

What does it feel like to feel really good about ourselves? If you ask a lot of people, you will most likely be very surprised

Feeling Good

by some of the common responses. 'I don't really know. It's ... it's so long since I felt really good about myself that I can't remember'. Do these sorts of replies sound typical? You bet they do!

Unfortunately few people have that spark that makes them feel good about themselves, where the problems of their world disappear, where the frustrations of other people suddenly don't seem to matter any more. And don't such people really annoy the hell out of the rest of us?

Yet this is not a world of make believe, of fantasies, or dreams without any realities. Change the way you feel about yourself, and you will suddenly change the way you see the world, and you will notice big differences in the way the world looks. Remember that couple at the restaurant I mentioned earlier? I would say without doubt that both those people had serious problems, not with the world, not with other people who were doing their best to serve them right, but trouble with themselves.

How do you feel about yourself? How do you see yourself?

How you see yourself has a lot to do with your self image. How you feel depends a lot on how you see yourself.

Look in the mirror once more. What do you see? Do you see lines at the sides of your eyes caused by lots of laughter? Do the lines around your mouth show where you have smiled a lot?

Or do these areas show no signs of laughter, of past smiles, past reasons to be happy with yourself, in yourself?

Look at yourself again, either picturing yourself in your mind, or take another look in the mirror. Now smile. Keep that smile. Try to feel good. Is it hard? Well, it shouldn't be.

In Your New Image

THERE'S LOTS TO BE HAPPY ABOUT ... IF YOU WANT TO BE HAPPY

When you have developed confidence in yourself, when you have improved your self image, then it is time to look at the ways you can be a happy person.

It is, of course, important to have lots to be happy about. One cannot force this emotion—that won't fool anyone, especially your subconscious mind. But try to look at all the events in your life that have brought just that little bit of pleasure. Picture them and hold those moments for a little longer. Relive them. What else made you happy? What happened last time that made you laugh? Then relive that moment in your mind, hold that image for as long as you can, recalling that event as clearly as you possibly can.

Now list a few more incidents that have made you happy—very happy. List every one of them—merely jotting down the event will suffice, because you will recall the rest of the details as you require them. But for now, recall everything that has made you feel pleasantly warm and jovial. Was it the good company you were with? Was it the feeling you got from being a success at some function? Was it passing an examination? All these are events in most people's lives that will usually evoke some feeling of pleasure.

Picture each of these events and hold the image clearly in your mind.

Elsewhere I have suggested very strongly that you should not dwell on the unpleasant incidents. Well, here, briefly, I intend contradicting that request to ask this of you for the only time.

List all the events—big and small—that have brought you no pleasure at all. I appreciate that some of these are important to you, even though they do evoke unpleasant memories. But, those general ones you could cut off from yourself and never need to bother with again, they are the ones I am asking you to recall.

List them. Then picture yourself standing on a high bridge over a fast flowing river, the river taking the water and everything in its flow far out of sight, far out to sea.

RIDDING YOUR LIFE FOREVER OF THOSE UNNECESSARY PROBLEMS

Picture yourself now wrapping up those troubles of yours that have brought no joy and happiness. Wrap the bundle up tightly with a good strong rope. See yourself there on the bridge, a huge bundle in front of you, a rope around the top to keep them all together. In your picture, tie that rope extra tight so the bundle does not undo itself on the course you are going to send it.

Now check in your mind that all those problems, those events, those incidents, are all there, tied together. Picture them clearly, be convinced that they can never escape from that bundle you have tied together.

Now see yourself throwing that huge bundle into the water. Picture this clearly. You should be able to picture this so clearly you can almost hear the splash it makes as it hits the water far below.

Now see this bundle of troubled times sink due to its energy as it hits the water, then float to the surface, to be picked up by the current.

Now watch it, in that picture in your mind, flow with the current, getting smaller and smaller as it recedes from your view.

Feel the load lifting from your mind as that bundle and all its contents disappears into the distance. Picture them going through the mouth of the river and out to sea, never to return.

Does this sound far-fetched and ridiculous? Let me reassure you this works! Dozens of people, just like yourself, have got rid of their troubles just by using this technique repeated over and over in their minds.

In Your New Image

But like all visualisation, those pictures have to be so clear and vivid you could honestly say you are on that bridge throwing that bundle of troubles into the river.

Don't picture them once and say, 'So what? I still have those problems. It didn't work'. Of course it won't work if you throw the bundle away only once. But every night for three or four weeks, every morning as you wake up, for three or four weeks? After a month of throwing your bundle of troubles into the river twice a day, you will most likely be feeling they were never around you to bother you previously.

If this seems too ridiculous, it will mean that you are saying that and, worse still, believing it because you have not honestly tried it. Well, try it and see what the difference is.

You will feel a load lifting from your mind. I won't say at this stage you will necessarily feel happy, but you should certainly start to feel less weighed down.

RIDDING YOURSELF OF YOUR PROBLEMS AND WORRIES IS ONE THING ... NOW RID YOUR LIFE OF YOUR GUILT

Perhaps it's time to shed some more of those troubled times. You won't be able to abandon the events, but you can certainly rid yourself once and for all time of the guilt and the unpleasant feelings associated with such events that have caused you so much anguish. Together, all such events weigh quite a bit, and that is indeed a heavy load to be carrying around with you.

So picture yourself on that bridge again, but this time put a whole lot of different, unpleasant emotions into that bundle. Picture the event, see in your mind detaching your emotions from each event just as you would tear off the leaves from a corn cob, and throw the emotions (symbolised by the corn cob leaves) onto the heap to form that new bundle.

Check them. Relive each event to ensure that you have stripped the unpleasantness from each of them in turn, and the unpleasant emotion is now in that bundle. Tie it. Tie it so tightly it will never never never come undone.

Like the bundle of problems, in your mind's image, throw it into the current of the river and watch it being carried into the distance and out of sight.

Feel it. That bundle has gone. Your load has been lightened once more, and just like the last bundle you threw away last month, this lot has gone forever.

Picture such an event twice a day—once in the morning and again just before you fall asleep—for three or four weeks. Remember, those unpleasant emotions have gone. They are no longer a part of your life.

Is it necessary to strip another load of troubled times of their husks and rid your life of them? You be the judge of this. If you were carrying around a lot of unhappiness and guilt, then it might be necessary to throw a few more loads into that current.

So what are you left with? Your troubles and burdens—most of them at least—have gone.

WITH THE UNHAPPINESS GONE, IT'S TIME FOR REAL LIVING

Without them you can concentrate on the good things in life. Those good things which give you a lot of joy might be small. Then so be it. To you, such events are the very important events in your life.

And the battle between good and bad thoughts is very much like a fight between a weak person and a strong person. It is nearly always the strong one who will win any round in a fight. And so too with good and ugly thoughts—it is nearly always the ugly thoughts that will dominate and overshadow those good, joyous events in our lives.

Having ridden your mind of this ugliness—an accumulation of a lifetime of things that you could not associate with happy emotions, you should of course be much better off.

But imagine what your life could be like from that moment on, not just without those unpleasant emotions, but instead having them replaced by lots of small moments of pleasure, of joy, of laughter, of feeling happy, of feeling good. That should put your emotions as far into the positive as the bad feelings previously put your emotions into the negative.

So now it is time to list events — and I don't care how far back in your life you have to go to find enough of them — that gave you a glimmer of pleasure, pleasure merely being defined here as an emotion that brought pleasant sensations.

List them. See them in your mind. Picture them clearly, one by one, as if they were happening right now. Hear the sounds associated with them. Make those images as real as you possibly can.

See them flow as if they are being relived on a conveyor belt, moving across one after the other in front of you. Watch them, feel the emotions you experienced with them at the time.

Now start reliving each of them twice a day. Again, I would suggest early in the morning soon after waking up, and just before you fall asleep at night. Make these moments part of your essential activities. They are more effective than any medication you could take that you think will make you feel happy. Medicines might help you feel less miserable and dull the senses. These positive images will make you happy!

After three or four weeks of getting rid of those burdens that weighed you down, your world would have been replaced by reliving incidents, all of which made you feel good at the time. How do you think you are going to feel from now on? Miserable? I doubt it. Nothing to be happy about now? I doubt it!

BRIGHTEN UP YOUR STYLE

It is often said that clothes make the person, and that the clothes we wear reflect the type of person we are. Look at a range of people you know. Do the unhappy ones wear bright clothes? Will an unhappy man wear a bright tie? Probably not. Will a happy man wear a bright tie? Yes, he most likely will.

Bright colours say one thing—hey, look at me. I feel good about myself. I don't mind if the whole world notices me. A person who feels less than happy is unlikely to wear bright colours because they do not really want the whole world to notice them. It is quite likely they will not want anyone at all to notice them. So they remain inconspicuous, trying their hardest not to stand out from others.

If you feel good about yourself, why not reflect your feelings?

It is unlikely that if you have endured many years of feeling less than happy you will suddenly feel comfortable wearing bright ties and scarves the next day. But if you see yourself in your mind wearing bright colours and feeling good about it, that will be quite a different result altogether.

You won't need to go to ridiculous measures to be able to wear brighter colours to reflect the way you now feel. Subtle changes, small changes one at a time will give you time to break yourself into accepting yourself in your new clothes.

This is how to enjoy life without those niggling, bothersome irritations ruling us.

ACTING—ACTUALLY BEING THE CHARACTER

Take a deep breath and let it out slowly and relax, and count to ten. Picture yourself in a peaceful setting for a minute or two.

Picture a character you would like to play—for a short time in real life, or in a play. You can, for this exercise, invent a person you would like to be for a while—or preferably identify someone you admire.

What does this person look like? How is he or she dressed? What are their movements? Are they fast or slow? Does the person use their hands a lot during conversation? Is the person you are picturing a nice person—strong personality, a good friend to a lot of people? What makes them different from perhaps all other people you could have invented or identified for this exercise? Is the character based on a person that you know well? Why did you pick this person?

Spend quite a bit of time creating this person—it could well be the person you would like to be.

Imagine yourself imitating this person. How do they stand? How do they speak? What is their voice like? Picture yourself (as this character you have invented) in conversation with a friend of this person. Imagine carrying on a conversation—listening, responding, listening, responding. More correctly, see yourself, as your imaginary character, reacting to this other person.

Now see yourself through another's eyes talking to someone on a bench in a park. What is the park setting like? Make it as realistic in your picture as you can. There should be sunshine, or rain clouds above, leaves on the trees, or fallen leaves on the ground. The picture you create must seem like a place you know.

What are the two of your doing? Are you facing this friend of yours? Are you listening intently? Is the wind blowing your hair gently into your face? Reality is important. Watch this scene of you and your friend in conversation for several minutes.

Now see the same scene through your own eyes, feel the air around you, listen to your friend's voice. This scene should be as real as if you were there with that person.

Now see yourself walking down the street through the city, as if you were this character you would like to be. Look at the people passing you. How do you feel? Do you feel tall? Do you feel proud of yourself? You should be—you have created this identity as you would like to be yourself. Are there many people around you? Do you feel comfortable in the presence of so many people, like the character you have created should feel?

Hold this scene for several minutes before moving on to the next one.

Feeling Good

See this character you have created (again, this is the person you would like to be, acting the part in life that you would like to play) doing something outstanding—swimming a long distance, running fast in an important race, taking on the role of an important actor in a movie. Watch the person in your picture not just begin the race, but watch that person—or more correctly, you—running that race at an outstanding pace, watching, seeing every step the person takes. If the person is swimming one kilometre, feel the power of each stroke. See every stroke. Imitate each stroke in your mind. If the person is jumping hurdles, see that person, really be that person, as they jump every one of those hurdles. Jump them yourself in your mind higher than they have been jumped before. Feel excited.

Create more and more images of yourself as the character you would like to be, reacting to everything that life throws at you in the way your character would react to those same situations. Give your character a range of tasks that you would envy in your hero. Make sure they are performed well and you are proud of your character for doing them so outstandingly.

As you watch your imaginary character acting, so you too should act the part of this person, imitating the actions that you like, speaking in the same way, possessing the same air of confidence that the person is lucky enough to have.

As you react to situations, you will find that these same mannerisms transfer to your own actions and the way you behave. This is why it is essential for this exercise to create a character that you really admire, one whom you wish you could really be. Not everyone can be in the Hollywood movies, but reacting in a confident manner at the right time on all occasions, and in social situations, will give you more to be proud of than being an actor in a movie. A movie lasts a little over an hour. Life lasts forever.

Chapter 12 Being a Winner

Would you like to become a winner? Would you like to have as much respect for yourself, for your abilities, as you would like others to have for you? I think it is quite unnecessary to answer those questions. We all would like to be winners, to succeed in whatever we undertake, to be successful in the full meaning of that term as it applies to us. As mentioned elsewhere in this book, success is whatever you want it to be for yourself. But I think it is safe to say that success is also to achieve what we aim for.

Believing in ourselves, being sure of ourselves, is what a new self image is about. We see ourselves as successful. We become successful because of the way we see ourselves. We live the life that we continually imagine ourselves to lead. This, believe it or not, is just as important as improving our self image so we no longer look at ourselves in the mirror each morning and squint at what we see. It is a matter of looking in that mirror and realising that the face in front of you can achieve all that you set out to achieve today, tomorrow, and every day in the future. That face in the mirror can reflect anything, any mood, any feelings, any passions, that you want it to. It can feel unloved. It can feel dejected, because the owner of the real face believes, whether there is any reason to or not, that there is nothing to offer anyone. You can feel despondent about the image you see because it is not quite as you would like it to be.

Being a Winner

This is why visualisation can, and does, turn that negative feeling around and make you, the owner of that image, feel good about yourself. The saying that it's all in the mind, although simplifying the result tremendously, is nevertheless true. When we see that image as positive and successful, then the owner of that image will be just that. Unfortunately, not many of us see that image in the mirror as a truthful replica of our true selves. We see little blemishes that make us shy away from the real world. We see a frown and we decide that we do not like the wearer of that frown. So we do not like ourselves very much. If, however, we look in that same mirror one morning and decide, yes, that is the image of a person who has personality, who commands respect, who is brim full with confidence, is talented, is going places, then that person will be all that.

A MIRROR WON'T TELL LIES. WE DO THAT ABOUT OURSELVES

In most cases where we do not like what we see in the mirror, the results will be negative through a cascading effect. We decide, I don't like that image (here, the image does not have to be a mirror image, for the results are even more effective if that false image of ourselves is merely in our minds). So we don't like ourselves. We put ourselves down at every step along the road of life. And because we feel miserable about ourselves (and by this stage we have every reason to be gloomy about ourselves), this is the time when others will take advantage of our dim outlook on ourselves, and make comments that we take personally. That in turn makes us feel worse about all those things we believe we cannot do properly.

If we can get out of that cycle, then the world is, quite simply, turned over on its axis.

Think for a moment about that person looking in the mirror, but this time, think of the person, you, as having no preconceived notions about the wearer of that face. Are you immediately going to say, I don't like that person because ... and list numerous reasons why you will not like the wearer of that face? Of course not.

BE COMPLETELY UNBIASED ABOUT THAT IMAGE IN THE MIRROR

Let us take this argument one step further and look at that person sensibly. If that same person who today didn't like what he or she saw, looked in the mirror tomorrow and said, 'I see promise. I might have been wrong about that person. Hey, he or she isn't too bad a looking person after all. It's just that I was biased before this. But yes, I really can see some things in that face that I like. And hey, that person really does have hidden talents. I recall that person's ability to do something at work last month that no one else had thought of. And hey, another thing I remember ... that was the way the person helped colleagues when they were struggling over a problem in the office. Yes, I am sure I was wrong about this person. I'm going to give this person a second chance.'

What do you think your reaction would be? Do you think you would still convince yourself, no, they're just saying that about me to make me feel better. No you wouldn't. You would feel good about yourself. And that feeling of minor triumph would escalate in the days ahead and make you feel better. You would get things done more efficiently, and achieve more of what you wanted to do.

And that is the magical power of visualisation. It is taking a negative image of ourselves, and turning it around so we like what we see in ourselves, and that in turn cascades along to other activities. It won't take long from the moment the image begins to turn around to when the person can notice changes for the better.

Being a Winner

And isn't that what we should be aiming for? Success (as it applies to us at an individual level), progress, achievements? All this can be summed up in one word — success.

With the use of visualisation to turn around that negative image of us, no one should expect a miracle cure overnight. It is not a magic bullet that is going to cure all our ills by the time the sun rises in the east tomorrow morning. That old, negative image took probably a lifetime to form and develop.

How long it takes to begin showing positive results will depend on your attitude, how often you visualise the person you would like to be, and how strongly you visualise the desired changes.

I REMEMBER YOU ... WHATEVER HAPPENED?

For talking about timing to bring about those desired changes, I must again refer to that figure of a few weeks or so. If you are serious. If you are determined to bring about changes, no you won't wake up in the morning a new person. But within that period of a few weeks I keep referring to, your mind will have begun to accept those new images of yourself, and will begin to act upon them. The changes won't come into being at midnight on the twentieth day either, for you will notice that the changes are very gradual, almost imperceptible at first. And that is a good thing, because on top of a change in your self image, you will have enough to cope with without having to face a whole new you that you don't even recognise. Others will be able to get used to that slow, gradual change more readily than if you went into work on Friday and said to them, Look at me. I'm the new worker here today. My name's ... No, thankfully, other people will barely notice the changes as they come into effect. At best they will say to you one morning months or even years later, something like, 'I remember when you were shy, quiet, you stuck to yourself in the corner. Whatever happened?'

Confidence will get you everywhere. A friend of mine just oozes confidence. I have seen him perform remarkably well at meetings, where he takes control of the meeting, leads it, and everyone attending comes away feeling that he has done a marvellous job. When analysed, it is clear that he hasn't done all that he could have done. In fact, on closer inspection of how he got away with so much at the meetings is not because he knew more than the others, or was more capable, but merely because he had the confidence. This alone inspired trust in him from all his colleagues. It works! Try it when you have developed your new image.

GO ON ... SHOW THEM!

I once attended a function where a medical officer I know quite well gave a talk. The audience reacted favourably and with enthusiasm to every word that he said. He was, for the evening, almost a hero. But a few days later, other medical officers told me that much of what he was saying was quite inaccurate. It wasn't what he was saying that instilled so much confidence and enthusiasm in his colleagues, but the way in which he said it. They, also medical officers with just as much medical knowledge, had not analysed what he had said at the time. They had been swayed by how he had got his message over to them.

This can be an asset too at interviews. Answering questions in such a way that it is obvious from your feeling of confidence that you know every bit as much as the interviewers, can often get you that job you want.

A friend of mine, one who likes to adopt the same cool, calm and confident approach to life as well as to interviews, recently was appointed to a senior position in a government service. He had the qualifications and the experience. And he had good referees' reports. His position before his senior appointment? He had been unemployed for nearly eighteen months! He was appointed over several who were more qualified, and who had

had just about, if not more, experience. Confidence had worked for him. It can, and will, work for you.

DON'T APOLOGISE FOR YOURSELF. BE YOURSELF!
The most dismal sight in our society is that of the person who apologises for his presence, speaks in a quiet voice so no one can hear him, approaches quietly, says nothing, and leaves as quietly as if he had never entered the room. He says little, but his behaviour says it all. This person is shy, a nightmare to himself.

It is surprising how many people just like that have, almost without exception, through visualisation only, turned around that extreme self image they have had and become outspoken, vocal and leading what can be termed pretty normal lives — a complete contrast to their former selves over only a matter of a few weeks or months. For them, a lifetime of being withdrawn had been reversed. They had come out and begun to live. It is people like these who make that dramatic transformation who realise, quite late in their lives, that there really is a big, beautiful world beyond their self image that they can enjoy as much as anyone else who wants to do so.

So how are you going to transform that mild-mannered self and become superman? The first step is to identify all that there is about you that you don't like today. No, not last week or when you were five years of age, but right now! List the aspects of yourself that you would like to change. Immediately you have identified them, write the positive corollary. You should not have to refer to that negative list again. If you don't like your face because you frown a lot, it is sufficient to merely write it down on that list, remove that frown and begin smiling. Suppose you do not like the way you speak — you might have a soft, quiet voice. For this point, it is sufficient to merely write 'speak loudly and confidently'. For the way you forget things that are important to you (and no doubt to others as well), write

In Your New Image

'I want to remember all the things that are important to me at work and to my family.' If you slurp your soup at home to the infuriation of your partner, simply write on the list, 'drink my soup quietly and cleanly without the need to wear a bib.' So do you see that it is not necessary to dwell on what you see as the negative aspects of yourself?

For the changes you need to bring about to become successful, to be a winner, your image of yourself has to be that of a successful person. You may well be surprised to learn through your own experience as you practise the exercises more and more, that it is possible to see yourself as a winner merely by seeing yourself in your image associating with successful people, to see yourself at a party, or at a function, with those in our society who are considered to be successes in their own fields of endeavour. This, really, can be seen as taking a short cut along the road forward, to see yourself already there, and not needing to take any side tracks along the way. But my advice is that you should overcome the aspects of your personality that you see as shackles, rectify them, move on, rectify the next one, take your time, then move on along the road to success slowly, surely, and succeed at every step in your new journey. You will not only overcome many of the traits that you identify as shackles, but you will also sense that feeling of success as you progress.

It is also important to not only list those traits that you see as your shackles, but also to think about all the traits that you would have if you were successful, and a winner, right now. You would quite possibly speak loudly (without shouting), confidently, face the person you are talking to and look them in the eye as you speak. You would be relaxed, self assured, realise your own abilities, hidden as well as the obvious. You would quite likely have good communication skills, be a good worker, dedicated, and freely associate with other people who have already reached that same degree of success that you are now able to aspire to. These are the images that you should strive for.

But shortly we will look at some individual ideas that will help you identify and work on the images of your new self that you want to create.

WHAT'S YOUR STIMULANT?

It is a sad fact of life that all the best intentions in the world can come to little, all the best self images can bring no results, unless we are able to motivate ourselves into action. For each of us, the stimulant to bring forward the motivation can be about as personal as success is to others. For some, boredom can be the greatest stimulant since the discovery of endorphins (those naturally occurring stimulants secreted by the brain). We know that if we don't change, we are stuck where we are. That thought that every day is going to be about as unexciting as today was, will soon get us up and running on all cylinders and at full power. But without any motivation, without an ability, without an incentive to motivate ourselves, we might remain as unchanged as we have up to this point. Without motivation, tomorrow is, well, how did you enjoy today?

But we need not always be unmotivated. If we don't have that stimulant as powerful as endorphins, the personal drive of a powerful locomotive, then all the good self images in the world won't, on their own, remove that inertia. Visualisation ... well, you guessed it!

One trait of nearly all successful people — the 'winners' — is that they get a lot done. If they have half an hour to spare, they do not go and make a cup of coffee because there is insufficient time to get anything else done. No, that half an hour is time they put to good use in getting ahead.

And those same people get up early and get moving. Possibly you have advertised an item for sale in the weekend 'for sale' classified advertisements in the newspaper. If you have, you could easily have observed a trend. Between seven and nine o'clock on the first day, you will get several telephone calls asking for information about the item you have for sale. And then, after about nine, possibly ten o'clock, calls will decrease. In the afternoon, you will get a lot more calls from those who have just got around to looking to see what they can buy. Then on the second day, you will get a lot of calls—from those who have just got around to reading the paper for that item they must have. During the week, you are likely to get a lot more telephone enquiries from people who were hopeful of picking up anything the motivated people didn't want. But of the people who rang during the whole of that period, those who rang you before nine o'clock were the more dynamic people— those who got things done, who got on in life. And those who trailed at the end of the line? Well, they are the people who have old cars, rent a small apartment because they will never be able to get further ahead.

By changing your habit, by getting going early in the day, and by putting your spare moments to good use, you will soon be able to acquire the habits of successful people—the winners. I am not suggesting that successful people never stop. I am not trying to imply that recreation, relaxation and moments for deep thought are not part of their lives. I am suggesting that too much of that procrastination, that time wasting, is harmful, although a little bit of it is good. If you do enjoy that cup of coffee while you lose yourself in your deep thoughts, or take that stroll around the block or through the park while you contemplate a problem, this is beneficial. So is reading a book. Or talking to your friends and family on the telephone—for a reasonable time. But just doing these things because you cannot see that there is sufficient time to start anything else, well, that's different. Remember, once you have changed your habits and you spend your time more productively, all these traits become your new habits, and it will be hard for you to go back to your time-wasting old ways. And what you will be able to achieve in all those previously idle moments during a week will astound you. The old saying that some people get ahead in the time that others waste certainly applies to anyone. And through visualising yourself with your new habits, you too can become a winner.

An important component in changing our self image is to put the new self image to good use. And with visualisation, here is that stimulant more powerful than that locomotive. We merely see ourselves doing! We see ourselves on the move. We see ourselves achieving whatever it is that we want. We see ourselves building up steam to move mountains and enjoy every rock that we are able to move. We see things in our minds, not as they are right now, but as we would like them to be, or as they could become. We can, through visualisation, make things move for us, make ourselves move. We should see ourselves getting every last bit of life out of our days, enjoying them to the fullest, appreciating every moment. And we won't get much out of any day if we are not moved, if we do not act on the power within us that we now have, or will soon have developed.

Without motivation, but with all the other good things about us in place—our self image, our newly developed talents, our expanded ideas about our capabilities—will lead to endless frustration unless we now do important things with those skills, talents and traits that we have developed. Unmotivated minds are like having that powerful locomotive all steamed up capable of doing great things with its power, but leaving it idle on the tracks to rust away. The human mind, although not made of a ferrous metal, can still almost rust out. Frustration caused by lack of motivation is worse in many ways than not having developed those talents. At least if we didn't know we had those talents, those new and great personality traits, we would not feel frustrated and disappointed. Motivation. Make it more powerful than that steamed up locomotive. Make boredom a stimulant that is more powerful than anything created on earth. You owe it to yourself to move yourself now that you can, now that you know how to.

In Your New Image

I have added this chapter near the end so that, hopefully, you will identify other traits that you want, or see the need, to sort out before becoming an instant winner. But, order is not really important, for I believe if you feel a success, you will be a success, and those other little things that bothered you will become so insignificant that either they won't bother you after a few weeks, or they will disappear and you will soon have forgotten them anyway.

BEING A WINNER

For this exercise, you will picture a number of scenes in which you excel and stand out from the crowd. Follow this exercise carefully, and you will really stand out in real life!

Take a deep breath and let it out slowly and relax, and count to ten. Picture yourself in a peaceful setting for a minute or two. Now see yourself at your place of work. Imagine the board room where a small meeting was planned for your section or department.

See yourself with the others from your place of work. What are they doing as they wait for the chairperson of the meeting? Are they talking amongst themselves? Are they scribbling on pieces of paper? Create this scene as vividly as you can.

Look around the room at the others, and hold this scene for a couple of minutes. Now, through another's eyes, see yourself take charge of the meeting. In your picture of yourself, you take a deep breath, relax quickly, and announce in a strong voice something to the effect that as the chair looks to be late, perhaps you could start the meeting.

See yourself conducting this unscheduled meeting, and notice the others at the meeting taking in what you are saying, and responding eagerly to your dialogue.

Hold this scene of you chairing this important meeting, talking, listening and asking questions, for at least five minutes.

Being a Winner

Picture yourself sitting in your comfortable chair again. Now picture a scene where your supervisor has scheduled a meeting with a client, but your supervisor has not turned up for this crucial meeting.

Through another's eyes, see the two of you introduce yourselves, and shake hands. What is this client like? Is he large and plump? Is she small and petite? What are they wearing? Are they carrying a briefcase? Do they wear spectacles? Create a picture that is almost real.

In your mind's image, see yourself boldly take charge of this embarrassing situation, and see yourself—hear yourself—ask the client into your supervisor's office.

Picture yourself sitting at the table in your supervisor's office, opposite the client, and watch this person open his or her briefcase and take out a folder of papers.

See yourself go to your supervisor's desk, search for the folder of papers that were to be the core of the discussion, and start talking to this person.

Hold this scene in your mind of you in full control for at least five minutes, hearing the conversation, seeing your client's movements vividly.

Through another's eyes, watch this scene for perhaps another five minutes as you talk, gesture with your hands, and speak in a loud, clear and confident tone.

Picture your supervisor entering the office, and you introduce him or her to the client. The three of you sit down at the table and resume the discussion.

Return to your comfortable chair for a few minutes and ensure that you are both physically and mentally calm and relaxed, free of all physical and mental tension. Pay special attention to the muscles in your legs, arms, back and neck. You want to be as physically relaxed at this stage as it is possible to get.

Picture yourself at your desk, and a person has just come in for a scheduled interview for a position your firm advertised recently. However, imagine a scene where those who were supposed to conduct the interview have left the building and cannot be located. See yourself take charge of the situation and save the firm from embarrassment.

Picture yourself showing the interviewee into the room and indicating a chair to sit in.

Now picture yourself finding a couple of other senior people in your firm, explaining what has happened, and asking if they will stand in for the others. Suggest that you would like to be present during the interview too.

Through another's eyes, see yourself conduct the interview, explain to the interviewee what the job involves, and explain the functions and the structure of the firm to this person.

See how the interviewee responds to your confidence. See the person answer your questions well, and notice how the person responds to the questions of the other senior staff.

How does it feel to have not only taken charge of the interview and conducted it, but also to have saved the firm, and your supervisor, the embarrassment of their absence?

In the real world, life is full of incidents where an individual, like yourself, can save the day for your firm, save embarrassment, and make one's self noticed by those who matter, such as management of your firm.

Not many people would be able to react as you have just pictured, so not many people stand out. If, however, you are prepared, and you act like a winner, you will be noticed — the others certainly won't be — and you will be able to take charge of events, big and small. If you rehearse such events well before they are likely to happen, you will stand out like the winner you have just seen yourself to be.

It is important not to limit yourself to just one or two likely events. One or two of perhaps hundreds, maybe thousands of events just like these are likely to happen almost any day. Their range is limited by your imagination only, for even the most

Being a Winner

unexpected events are those that will happen with most frequency. Plan ahead, and be a winner!

PUTTING YOUR TIME TO GOOD USE

Take a deep breath and let it out slowly and relax, and count to ten. Picture yourself in a peaceful setting for a minute or two. Now see yourself in your mind's image looking at your watch or a clock and noticing that you have twenty minutes before you need to leave home or begin a large, time-consuming task. In your picture, see yourself considering what you can accomplish in those twenty minutes, or what you can at least begin without necessarily finishing the job. Now see yourself starting—hold this image clearly in your mind for a couple of minutes. You are, in your mind, aware that you have only a short time, but really want to begin the next job. Picture yourself beginning this.

Through another's eyes, watch yourself performing this task with full enthusiasm. In your picture, your clock is nearby but the idea here is to be aware that you are accomplishing something important in a limited time. You are not only beginning the task ahead of you, but you are actually working up to the next deadline that you have set for yourself.

In your picture, see yourself still performing the main task right up to the moment you have to leave it.

If you picture scenes like this vividly enough for the next few weeks, you will develop a new (and good) habit of using your free time constructively and productively.

STARTING YOUR DAY OFF EARLY

Take a deep breath and let it out slowly and relax, and count to ten. Picture yourself in a peaceful setting—on the beach or in a field full of flowers—for a minute or two. Now see yourself as you would normally get up on a weekend, whatever time that might be. In your image, look at the clock beside your bed and see that it is a few minutes before seven o'clock in the morning.

In Your New Image

Picture yourself stirring, stretching, and remaining there in the comfort of your warm bed until the hands of the clock go around to just on seven o'clock. Now, in your mind's image, see yourself throwing off the bed covers and stepping out of bed.

Through another's eyes, see yourself go to the kitchen or dining room window, and look at the sun rising and the dawn breaking outside. Hold that view in your mind for a couple of minutes, taking in the real beauty of the morning.

In your image, picture yourself eating breakfast and enjoying the taste of the food and the coffee.

Again, in your image, look at the clock again and notice that the time is only a quarter past seven.

Through another's eyes, see yourself getting showered and dressed and ready for the day ahead. Look at the clock and notice that the time is a little after seven thirty in the morning. You feel good, because you are now ready to begin your day, and the day is still very young.

In your mind, consider all the jobs you would like to do, and list them in the order that you would like to tackle them.

Through another's eyes, picture yourself beginning the first task on your list of duties for the day, and see yourself begin it, watching yourself not only begin, but working at it eagerly.

Now picture yourself starting the next task you have listed, and enjoying beginning that. Hold this scene in your mind for at least a couple of minutes. Now, in your mind's picture, look at that clock again, and feel good inside that you are onto the second task you have set yourself for the day, and it is only a little after eight o'clock.

If you picture scenes such as these, vividly and consistently enough for a reasonable time, this early rising and starting early in the day will become a habit that you will find rather hard to break. Consider how much more you can achieve in the same amount of time that you had before!

Chapter 13 Where To From Here?

Phew ... can I really change all those things about me?

Yes, of course you can. If you want to. The scenarios described throughout this book were selected because the subjects were those that I am most often asked to help people with. I believe they represent the attitudes and changes most readers will want to embark on in their own lives. Don't be alarmed by the wide variety of such scenarios. It is unlikely that most readers will consider more than a very small number applying directly to them. No book could cover every possible change every human being might want to bring about in their everyday lives.

You will have seen how changes can be brought about in your life with minimal effort on your part for substantial reward if you really desire such changes. You have seen how you can bring about changes in behaviour, sports performance enhancement, and how easy it is to go from a fumbling, mumbling employee to one who gets the job done, or gives a presentation that is meaningful and enriching. You have seen how to change your attitude and remove that shyness with people you meet who could quite likely become your friends.

But of course the possibilities don't stop there. If you can see a need to bring about any other changes, select one of the scenarios that is close to what you want to achieve, consider the right images you should form for the most beneficial results, and go for it.

In Your New Image

Instead of needing to increase your reading speed, increasing your keyboard speed might be more important. Then apply the same principles for that activity. Instead of learning how to weld or work with wood, you might prefer to take cooking classes and become an excellent cook. Instead of feeling uneasy with your boss, you might be a person who envies your friends when they communicate by touching—you consider that you are missing out on similar affection but cannot bring yourself to engage in touching others (such as hugging friends, shaking hands, patting your friends on the back to show that you are proud of them) as a mark of affection. Then select a suitable scenario and change the images (or devise your own scenario according to your needs) and overcome this in your life. Instead of wanting to make new friends, your more immediate need might be to develop patience. Then apply the same principles and overcome your impatience. Instead of working more on weekends, your priority might be to slow down. You will have worked out by now how to apply the rules to help you slow down.

Remember ... it's your life, you decide what you want to change, and go for it.

Good luck in your new image!

Index

Accepting ourselves	36, 104 - 109
Achieve all that you set out to do	12
Achieve the impossible	16
Achieving a goal	27
Acquire new skills	19, 116
Acting – actually being the character	173
Be a winning sports person	118
Be yourself – not someone else	69
Become the person you want to be	26
Being a winner	11, 176, 177, 179, 181, 183, 185 - 187, 189
Being sure of ourselves	12, 176
Belief is the secret	22
Believing in ourselves	12, 176
Brighten up your style	172
Broadcast on radio	15
Business presentations	153
Change your behaviour	15
Changing behaviour and attitudes	9
Childhood	20, 21, 40, 42, 69
Concentrate on the achievable	66
Conditional reflex	39
Create a new photographic album	52
Create the desired picture	9, 11
Create what you want in your life	44
Create your pictures	55
Creating images	8, 54, 61
Creating positive mental images	26

Creating the right positive images of ourselves	12
Cycling	55, 116, 123, 125
Dealing with difficult people	110, 111, 113, 115
Decide what is worth worrying about	164
Desired changes are possible	27, 46
Determine the improvements you want in your life	18
Don't limit yourself	27
Effective means to change your behaviour	11
Enhance what you are capable of doing.	16
Enhance your expertise in sports	19
Expected improvement	9, 11
Fear of animals	87
Fear of travelling	81, 85, 92
Feel good about ourselves	12, 166
Feel relaxed at taking examinations	15
Feel secure in the future	25
Focus on the desirable	46
Focus on what you want	33, 60
Forget the past	20
Freedom	24, 28-31, 34, 60
Get a picture of life	43
Give dynamic presentations	18
Golf	7-8, 19, 32-33, 116, 118, 124
Handicap	19, 160
Head in the right direction	28
How big are you?	105
Image in the mirror	12, 177
Interviews	19-20, 44-47, 51, 148-152, 187-188
Is the problem with you, or with the rest of the world?	74
It is what we believe that counts	47
It's time for real living	171
It's your idea. It's your business	135
Job security	25
Joy of victory	23
Jumping	100, 116, 125, 175

Learn to picture all your past successes in life	79
Learn to respect some fears	84
Learn to talk to people	142
Loneliness	158-160
Look ahead	31
Make something rewarding and satisfying of our lives	66
Making friends	158, 159, 161, 163
Most improvements are possible	121
Move your life forward	15
Moving ahead for achievement	138
Negative attitude	10, 17
Never give up	34, 86
New expectations of ourselves	66
New way of living	26
Opposite sex	19, 39, 58, 95, 158, 160
Overcome shyness	19, 89
Overcoming the conditioning	43
Patience	58, 192
People who succeed have a good self image	73
Picture a perfect day	33
Picture the changes you want	15
Placebos	22, 46
Poor self image	67-68, 73, 78
Practicalities of what you want to achieve	18
Practising in the mind	9
Prepare yourself for changes	37
Preparing for examinations	97
Public speaking	7, 19, 39, 87, 100, 103
Putting your time to good use	189
Reading faster	126 - 128
Regression	21
Relationships	25, 160
Relaxation	10, 54-55, 63-64, 79, 91, 95, 97, 101, 114, 184
Removing anxiety	81, 83, 85, 87, 89, 91, 93, 95, 97, 99, 101, 103
Rid your life of your guilt	170

Ridding your life forever of those unnecessary problems	169
Running	8, 55, 89, 115-116, 118-120, 125-126, 175, 183
See ourselves as capable, secure, confident individuals	66
See what you want	22, 137
See yourself for real	26
Seeing the possible	27
Self-confidence	8-9
Self-doubts	8, 10, 15, 17, 19, 23, 26, 31, 38
Self-fulfilling prophecies	26
Self-image	12, 26, 29-31, 37
Self-restriction	8
Self-satisfaction	28
Simplest thing to fool is our own mind	47
Sports performance	8, 9, 11, 191
Start small, end big	72
Starting your day off early	189
Stop procrastinating	143, 146
Surging ahead in your life	18
Survival of those best suited to their environments	131
Technique of creating pictures	49
Tennis	8, 32, 117-118, 124
There really is a bright future for you	134
Think differently ... Act differently	45
Tolerance	112
Traumatic events	21
Unblocking the barriers	26
Using creative imagery to improve performance	14
Using your imagination	44
Vision to realise what is possible	27, 70
What if ... What does it matter	40
What is achievable	36
What is achievable	17
What is victory	23
What you want to be and want to achieve	11, 18
Winning in the lottery of life	160

Work	144
Working for yourself	133, 137, 156
You must feel good about yourself	107

www.ingramcontent.com/pod-product-compliance
Lightning Source LLC
Chambersburg PA
CBHW060515090426
42735CB00011B/2232